Paper Airplanes MEGA PACK

Instructions to Fold Four Planes and Enough Paper to Make Hundreds of Gliders

Norman Schmidt

STERLING INNOVATION
New York

STERLING INNOVATION
New York

An Imprint of Sterling Publishing
387 Park Avenue South
New York, NY 10016

© 2014 by Sterling Publishing

This book is excerpted from the following Sterling/TAMOS titles:
Best Ever Paper Airplanes © 1994 by Norman Schmidt
Super Paper Airplanes © 1994 by Norman Schmidt

ISBN 978-1-4549-1232-3

Distributed in Canada by Sterling Publishing
c/o Canadian Manda Group, 165 Dufferin Street
Toronto, Ontario, Canada M6K 3H6
Distributed in the United Kingdom by GMC Distribution Services
Castle Place, 166 High Street, Lewes, East Sussex, England BN7 1XU
Distributed in Australia by Capricorn Link (Australia) Pty. Ltd.
P.O. Box 704, Windsor, NSW 2756, Australia

For information about custom editions, special sales, and premium and corporate purchases,
please contact Sterling Special Sales at 800-805-5489 or specialsales@sterlingpublishing.com.

Manufactured in China

2 4 6 8 10 9 7 5 3 1

www.sterlingpublishing.com

Contents

CONSTRUCTION TIPS 4

EGRET 6

PIPIT 9

SWALLOW 12

CONDOR 15

Construction Tips

When carefully made, the paper airplanes in this book are super flyers. They can be built using the paper included, or ordinary 20 or 24 lb bond copier paper. Bond paper is lightweight, easy to cut and fold, and easy to fasten together. It is available in a variety of colors (black paper may have to be purchased at an art store). Since a paper airplane's lift and thrust are limited, every effort must be made to keep drag at a minimum. Every surface not parallel to the direction of travel (wings, nose, and canopy) adds drag, so the neater and more accurate your construction, the better the plane will fly. Clean and accurate cuts and crisp folds are a top priority.

MEASURING AND CUTTING

Use a sharp pencil to mark the measurements and draw firm, accurate lines. Cut out pieces with a sharp pair of scissors or a craft knife and a steel-edged ruler. A knife makes a cleaner cut. When using a knife be sure to work on a proper cutting surface.

FOLDING

Always lay the paper on a level surface for folding. Folding is easier along a score line (an indented line on the paper made with a hard pencil drawn along a ruler). There are only four kinds of folds used in making the airplanes in this book. They are mountain folds, valley folds, sink folds, and reverse folds. Where multiple layers are folded, run your fingers back and forth along the fold, pressing hard to make a sharp crease.

GLUING

A glue stick works well for paper airplanes. Follow the instructions for gluing. Cover the entire contacting surfaces that are to be joined. If there are multiple layers, apply glue to each of the sheets. Glue should be used sparingly, but use enough to hold the parts together. Where multiple layers are being joined, you may need to hold the pieces for a few minutes until the glue sets.

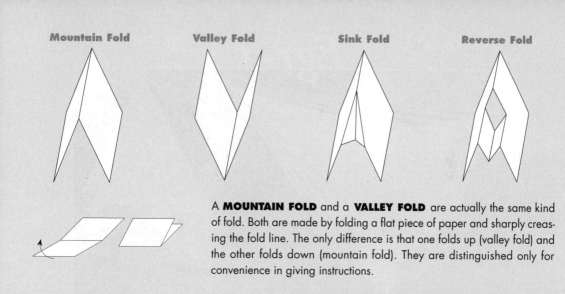

Mountain Fold   **Valley Fold**   **Sink Fold**   **Reverse Fold**

A **MOUNTAIN FOLD** and a **VALLEY FOLD** are actually the same kind of fold. Both are made by folding a flat piece of paper and sharply creasing the fold line. The only difference is that one folds up (valley fold) and the other folds down (mountain fold). They are distinguished only for convenience in giving instructions.

To make a **SINK FOLD**, begin with paper that has been folded using a mountain (or valley) fold and measure as required across the folded corner. Then push in the corner along the measured lines, making a diagonal fold. Finish by creasing the folds sharply.

To make a **REVERSE FOLD**, begin with paper that has been folded using a mountain (or valley) fold and measure as required, down from the top and in from the edge. Then cut along line from the top (heavy line). Push cut piece in, as shown. Finish by creasing folds sharply.

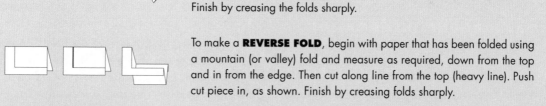

5

Egret

BACKGROUND INFORMATION

This airplane is called the "Egret" because of its slender shape and long nose. It is a delta (triangle) wing design. The plane looks like a flying triangle. Delta wings are used in slow-flying planes such as hang-gliders and high-speed planes such as the Concorde, which carried passengers faster than the speed of sound. Delta wings will probably be used in future planes that will carry passengers into space and back.

6

TECHNICAL INFORMATION

The Egret is constructed similarly to the common paper airplane that everyone makes. But because of this model's carefully measured shape, it can attain a very smooth and flat glide. Make sure that its shape is properly adjusted, with vertical tails straight up and down. Hold it between thumb and fore-finger, launching it gently straight ahead.

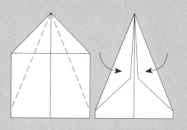

STEP 2 Valley fold the upper diagonals along broken lines to meet the center crease.

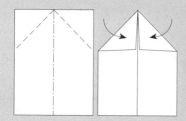

STEP 1 Lay paper flat in a vertical direction. Fold paper in half vertically using the mountain fold. Unfold. Then valley fold the upper corners to the center crease.

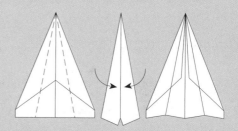

STEP 3 Valley fold outer edges along broken lines to meet the center crease. Unfold, as shown.

7

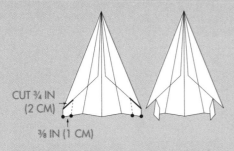

CUT ¾ IN
(2 CM)

⅜ IN (1 CM)

STEP 4 On each side, measure along diagonal edge of the paper, as shown by heavy line, and cut. Measure along bottom edge, in from each wing tip, and from this point, draw a line to the end of the cut. Valley fold along this line to make vertical tails.

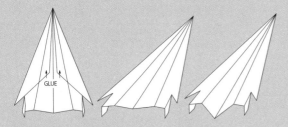

GLUE

STEP 6 Glue folds only at the center of fuselage. Flip airplane over. Adjust shape so that when viewed from the back, the airplane makes a shallow upside-down W, as shown.

STEP 5 In the locations shown, measure, cut, and fold the elevators.

ELEVATORS ¼ in x ³⁄₁₆ in (.6 cm x .5 cm)

CUT
FOLD
CUT

NOTE: In the instructions, control surfaces (elevators, ailerons, rudder) are shown in black. The cuts are always ³⁄₁₆ inch deep on ends only, but widths vary. Their dimensions are always written as follows:

⁹⁄₁₆ IN x ³⁄₁₆ IN (1.4 CM x .5 CM)
OR
¼ IN x ³⁄₁₆ IN (.6 CM x .5 CM)

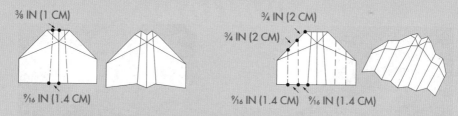

⅜ IN (1 CM)

⁹⁄₁₆ IN (1.4 CM)

¾ IN (2 CM)

¾ IN (2 CM)

⁹⁄₁₆ IN (1.4 CM)   ⁹⁄₁₆ IN (1.4 CM)

STEP 5 On each side of vertical center crease, measure and draw lines as indicated. Then mountain fold along drawn lines, as shown. Measure and draw the next two sets of lines, on each side. Valley fold line A and mountain fold line B on each side, as shown.

GLUE NOSE ONLY

VIEW FROM BACK

STEP 6 Glue nose only, and let back flare open. Adjust so that, when viewed from back, it makes a shape as indicated.

Swallow

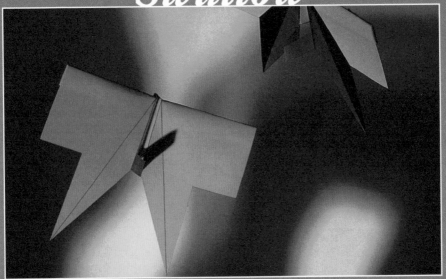

BACKGROUND INFORMATION

This airplane is called the "Swallow" because of its deeply forked tail, which resembles that of the bird. When airplanes were first invented, many different kinds of tails were tried. This is an interesting looking airplane. It can soar in a gentle breeze.

TECHNICAL INFORMATION

The Egret is constructed similarly to the common paper airplane that everyone makes. But because of this model's carefully measured shape, it can attain a very smooth and flat glide. Make sure that its shape is properly adjusted, with vertical tails straight up and down. Hold it between thumb and forefinger, launching it gently straight ahead.

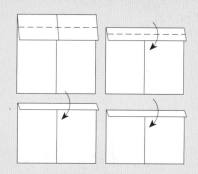

STEP 2 Valley fold the top again to meet the horizontal crease. Then valley fold the top again, to meet the horizontal crease. Finally, refold the original horizontal crease.

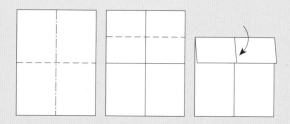

STEP 1 Lay paper flat in a vertical direction. Fold paper in half vertically using a mountain fold. Unfold. Valley fold the paper in half horizontally. Unfold. Then valley fold the top to meet the horizontal crease.

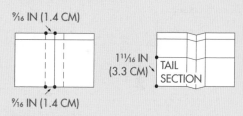

⁹⁄₁₆ IN (1.4 CM)

⁹⁄₁₆ IN (1.4 CM)

1¹¹⁄₁₆ IN (3.3 CM)

TAIL SECTION

STEP 3 On each side, measure from center crease and draw lines, as shown. Valley fold along these lines. Unfold. Measure from bottom along side and draw a horizontal line.

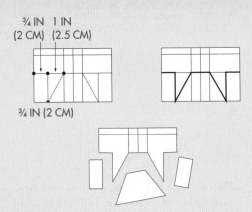

STEP 6 Measure, draw, and cut along heavy line at back of fuselage, as shown. Reverse fold to make the vertical tail (see page 5).

¼ IN (.6 CM) CUT

REVERSE FOLD

STEP 4 Measure and draw lines on tail section, as shown. Cut out along heavy lines, as shown. Discard cutouts.

¾ IN 1 IN
(2 CM) (2.5 CM)

¾ IN (2 CM)

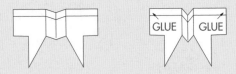

GLUE   GLUE

STEP 5 Reshape the airplane by refolding the vertical creases. At each wingtip, glue folded-over portion of the wing's leading (front) edge. Glue no more than $9/16$ in (1.4 cm) from each wingtip.

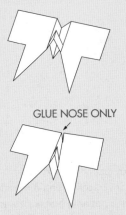

GLUE NOSE ONLY

STEP 7 Apply glue to the nose only, leaving the back to flare open. Adjust the wings so they are level in flight.

14

Condor

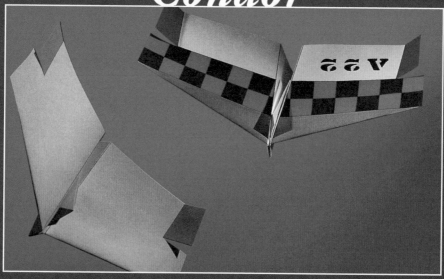

BACKGROUND INFORMATION

This airplane is called the "Condor" because of its large, broad wings. This design is a variation on a flying wing. Unlike conventional airplanes, this design has no horizontal and vertical tail. Winglets are incorporated into the wingtips, which provide both horizontal and vertical stability. Like all flying wings, it is sensitive to pitch control. The wide wingspan makes it quite fragile, and it should be launched gently straight ahead. It is not a windy weather airplane.

TECHNICAL INFORMATION

Condors have large feathers at their wingtips for control. Instead of feathers, this airplane has winglets. Because of its wide wingspan, this paper airplane is fragile where the wings meet the fuselage. Adjust the winglets and bend the airplane for trim adjustment.

STEP 1 Lay paper flat in a horizontal direction. Fold paper in half vertically using the mountain fold. Unfold. Then valley fold in half horizontally. Unfold.

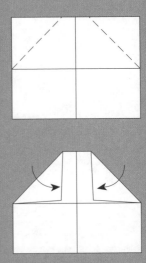

STEP 2 On each side, valley fold diagonally so that the outer edges meet the horizontal crease.

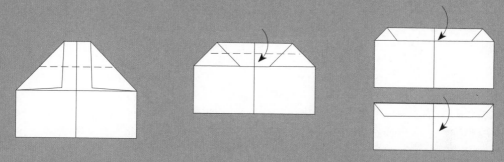

STEP 3 Valley fold along broken lines so that the top edge meets the horizontal crease. Valley fold again, so that the top edge meets the horizontal crease. Then refold the original horizontal crease.

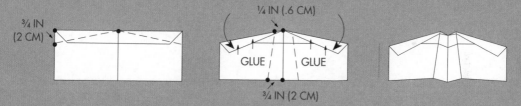

STEP 4 On each side of vertical crease, measure and draw diagonal lines. Valley fold top outer edges along these lines. Glue folded-over triangles to form the leading (front) edges of the wings. Then measure and draw vertical lines, as shown. Valley fold along vertical lines to form the fuselage.

STEP 5 Flip the airplane over. On each side, measure and draw lines for the winglets. Make horizontal cuts on heavy lines. Valley fold, as indicated, to make winglets. Make a canopy (type 2).

CANOPY (TYPE 2) 1 1/8 in x 1 11/16 in (2.8 cm x 4.3 cm) with top point 3/4 in (2 cm) from front tip

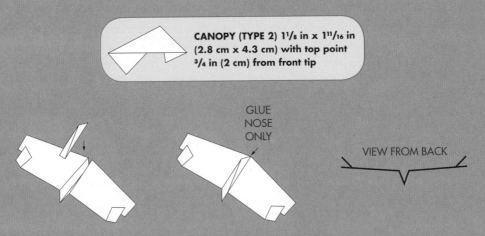

STEP 6 Apply glue to inside of nose only, and insert canopy. Align with nose. Adjust the shape so that the wings have a slight dihedral angle (upward slant) and the winglets slant upward, as shown.

18

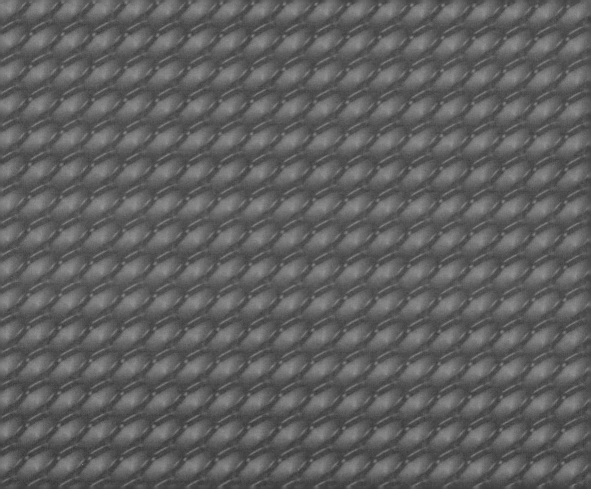

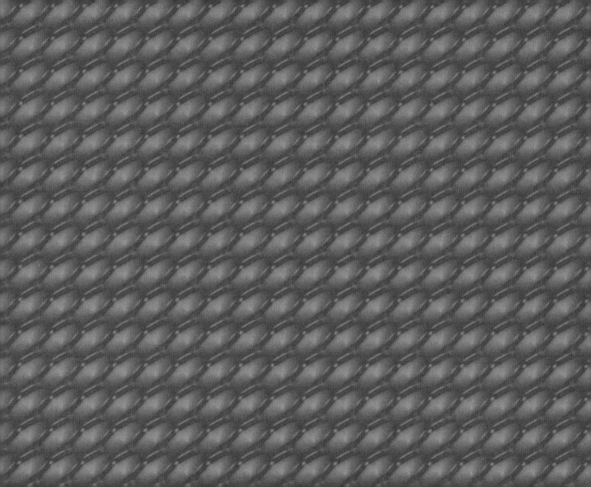

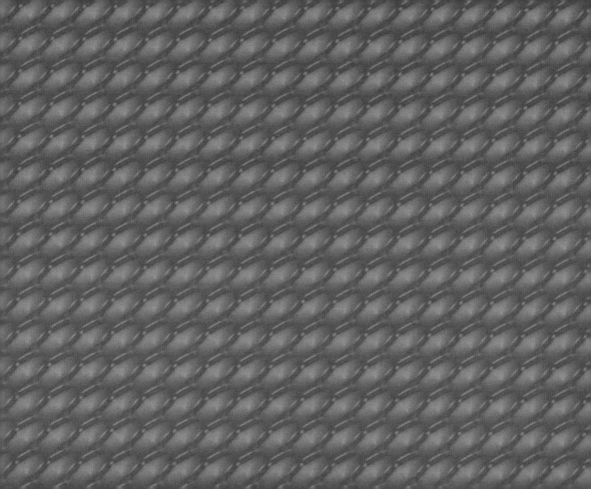

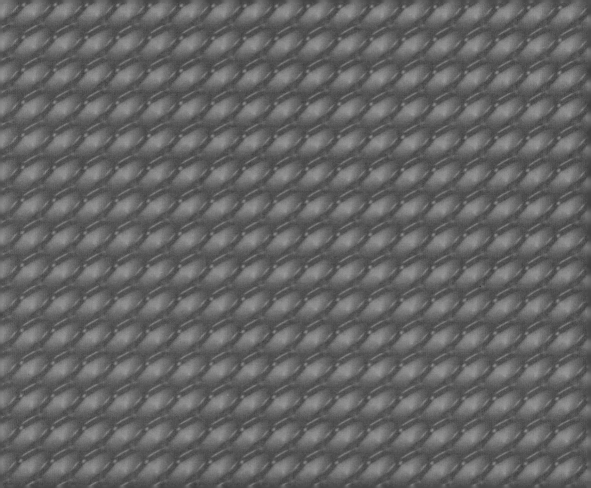

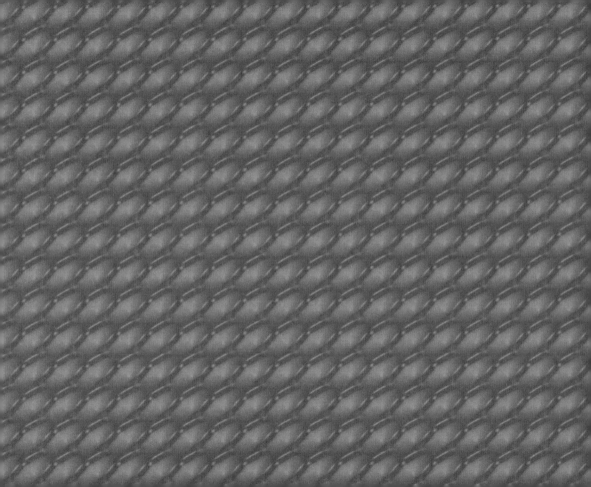

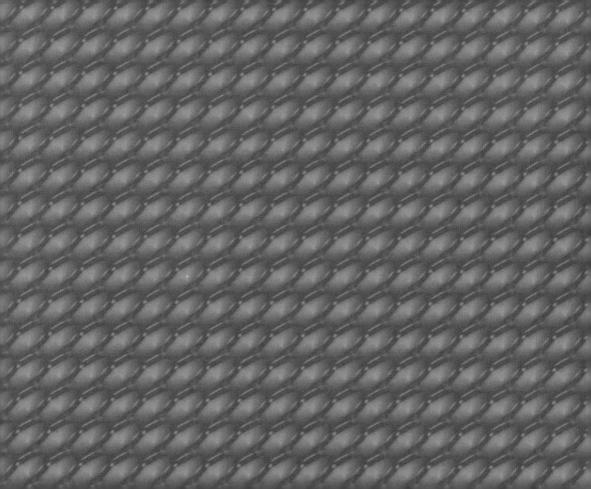

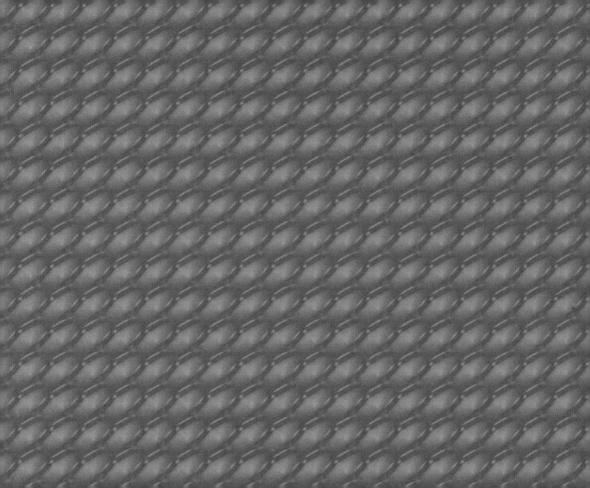

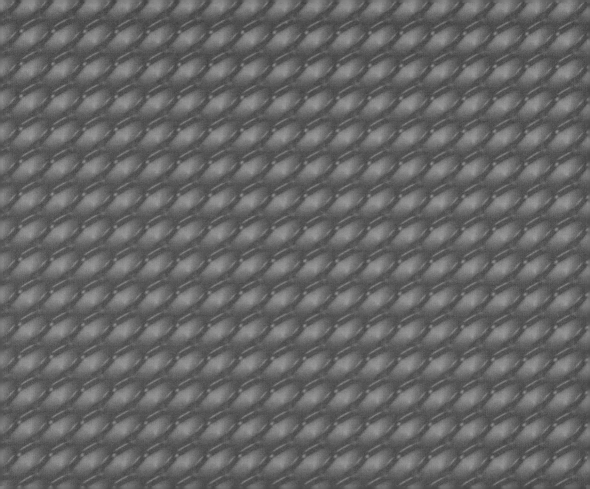

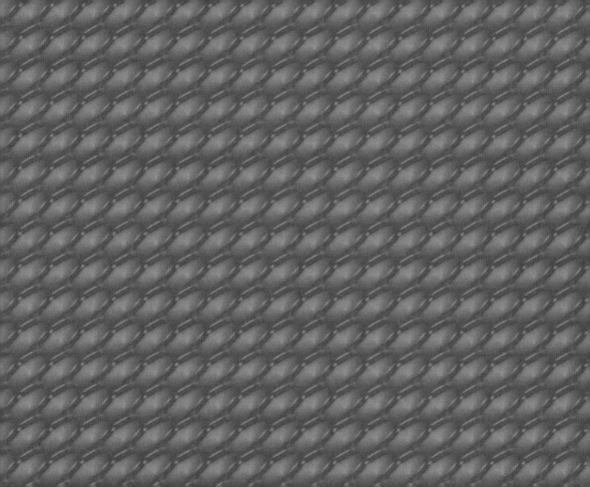

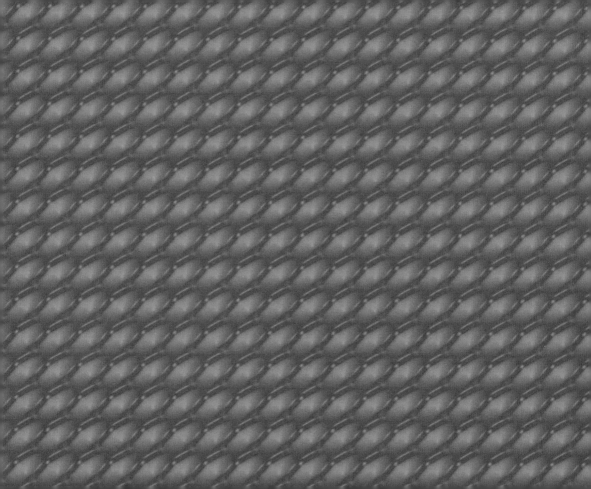

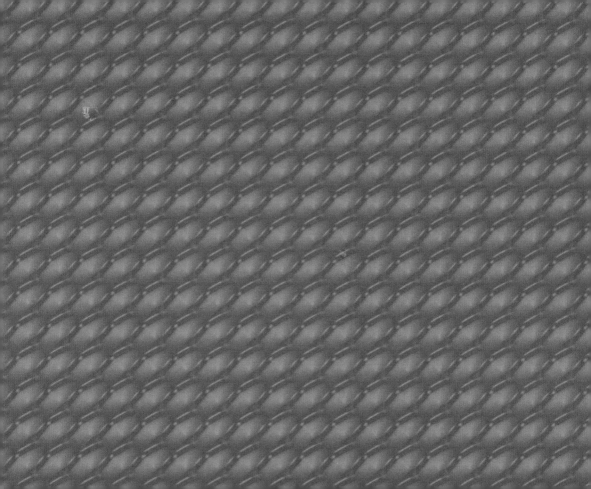

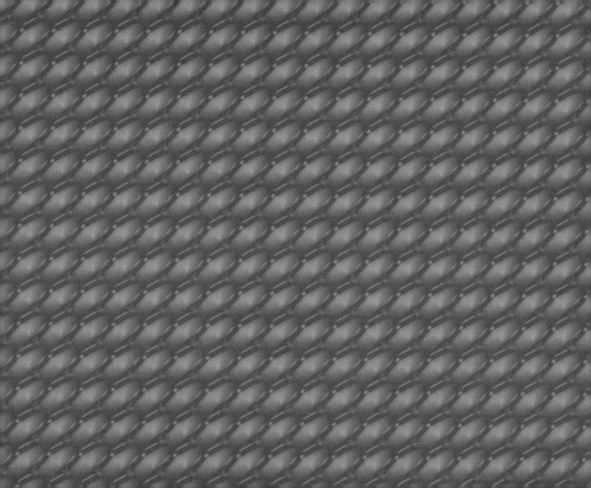

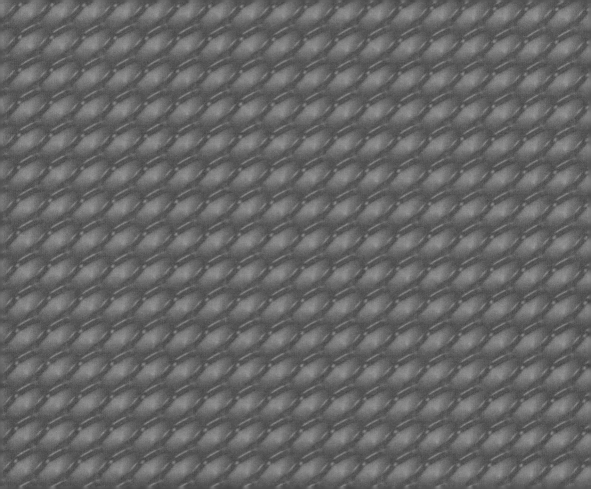

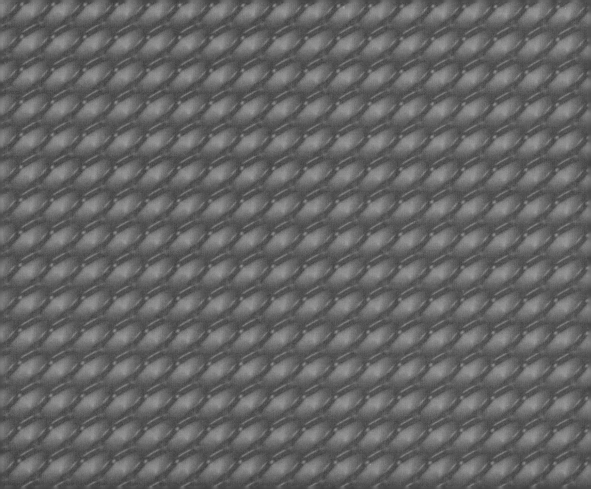

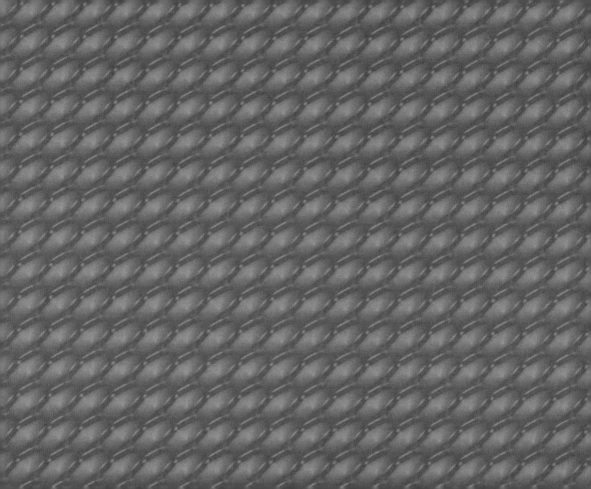

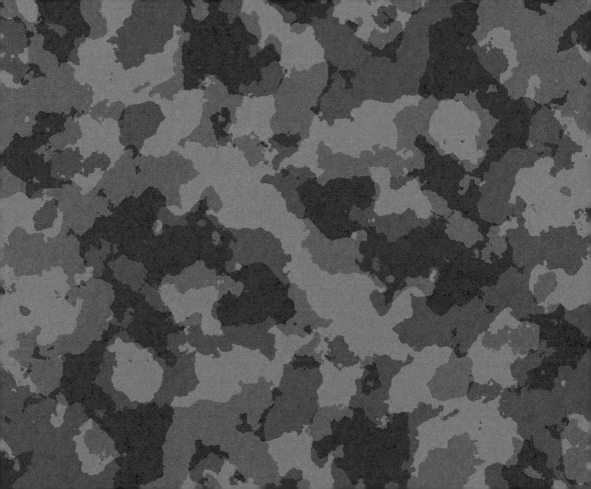

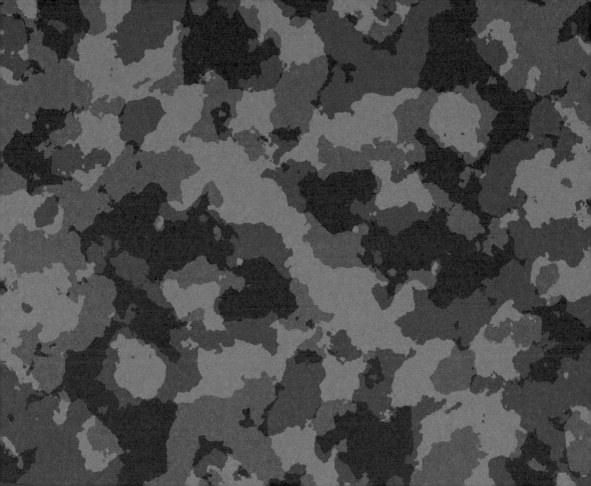

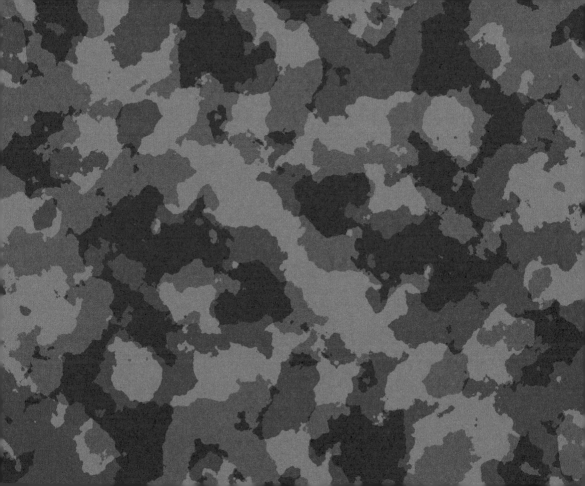

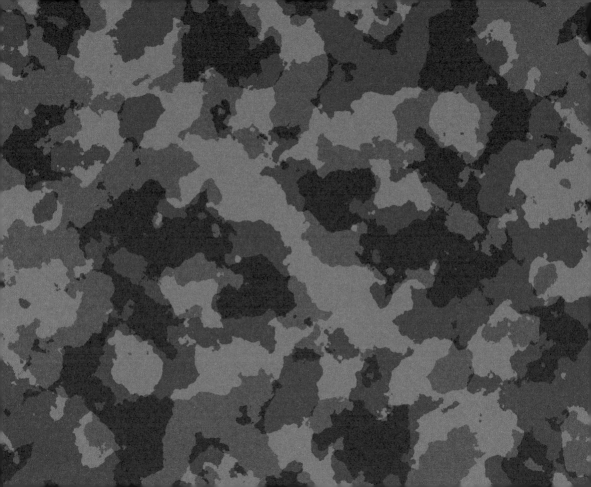

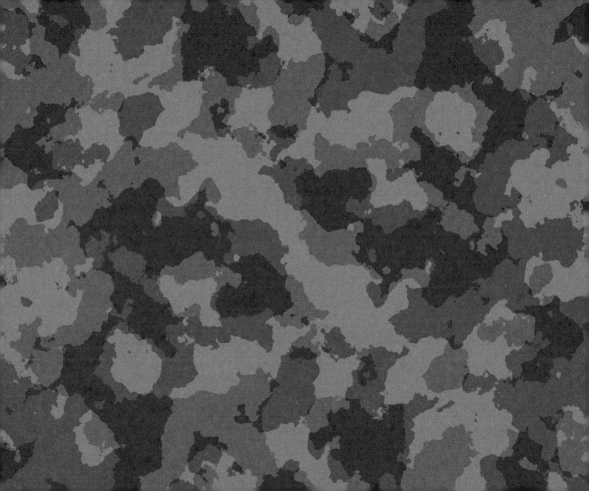

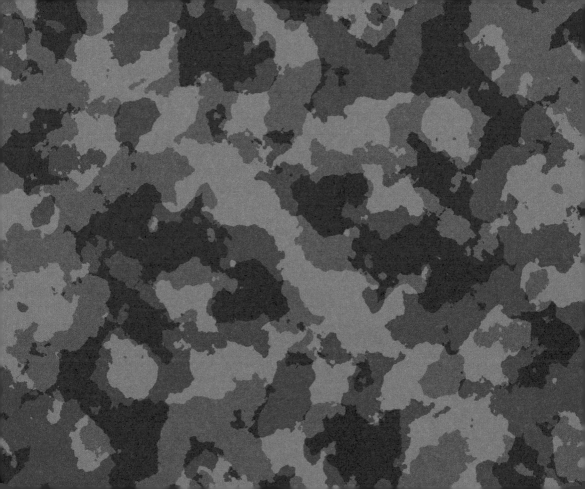

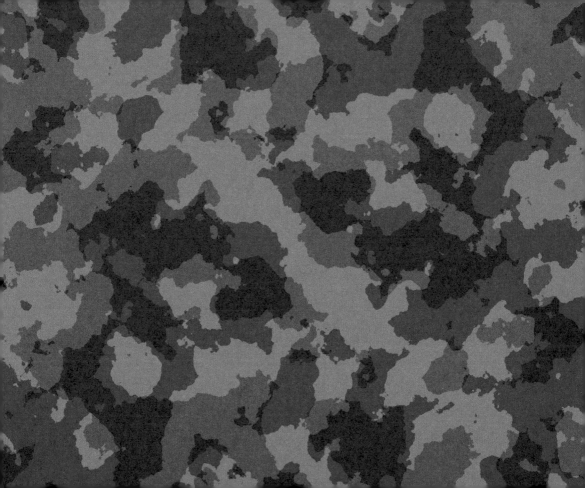

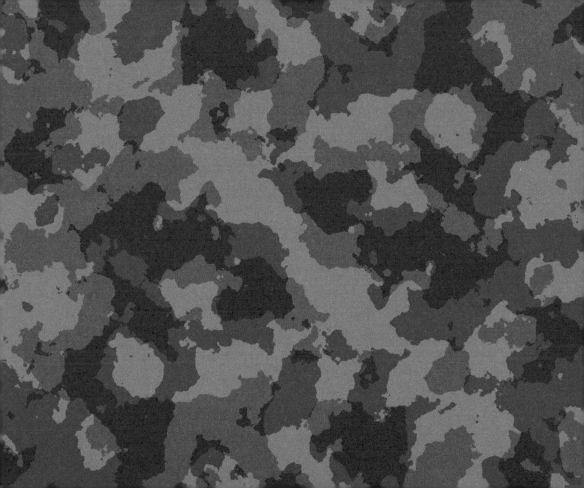

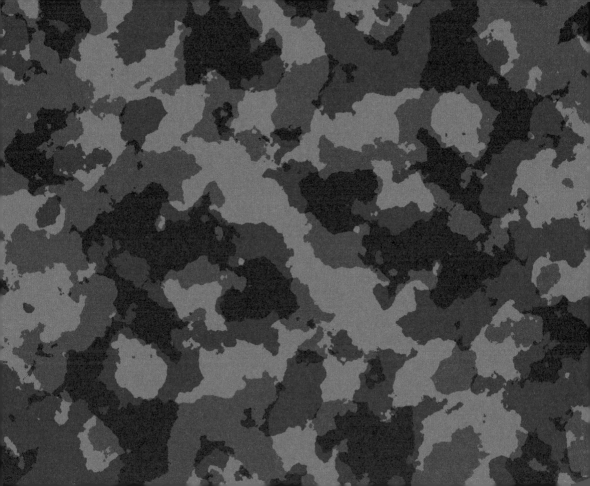

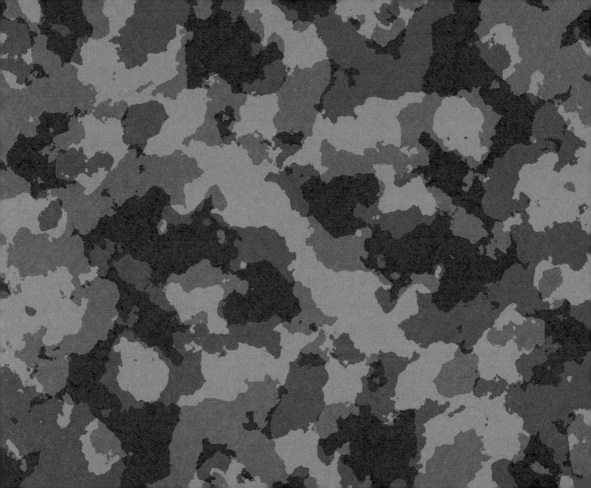

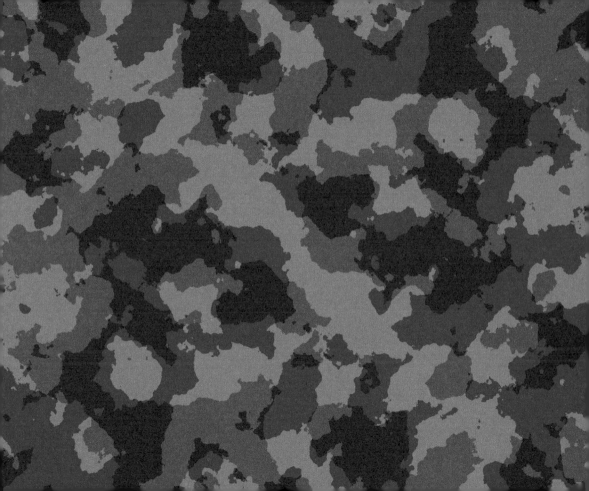

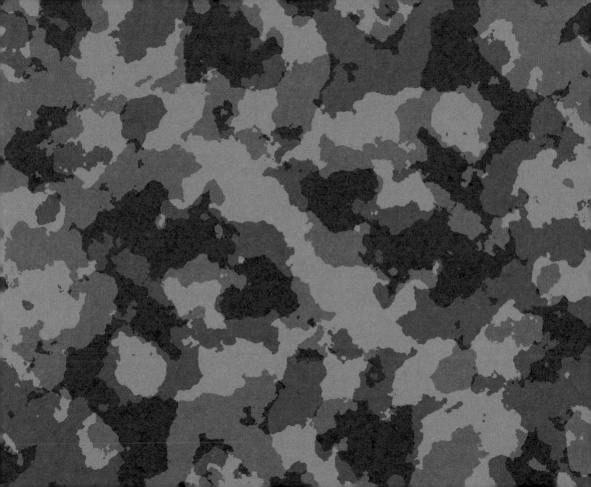

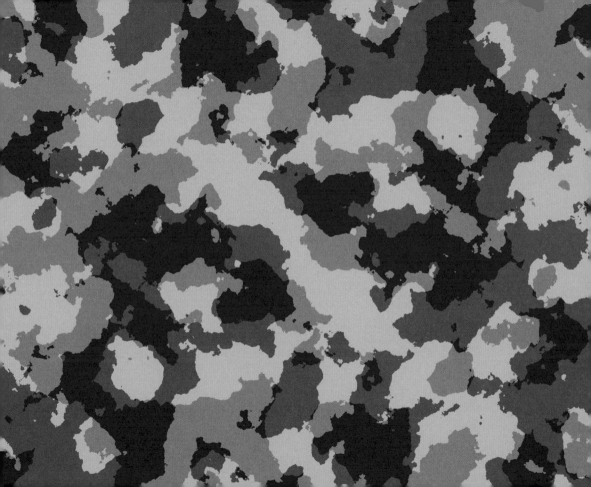

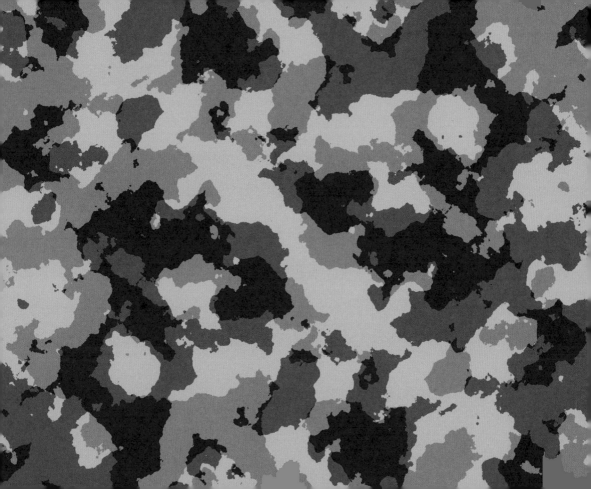

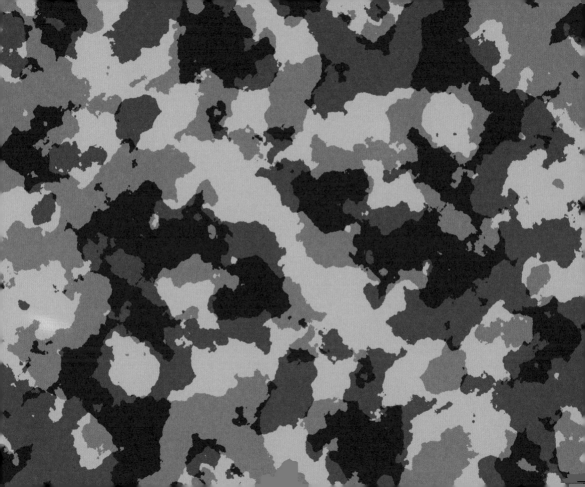

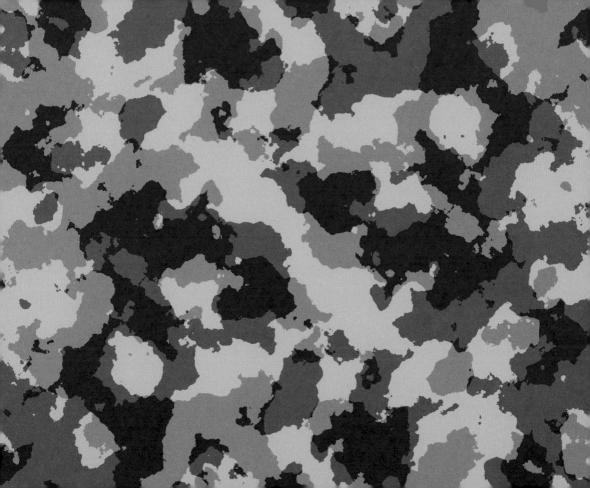

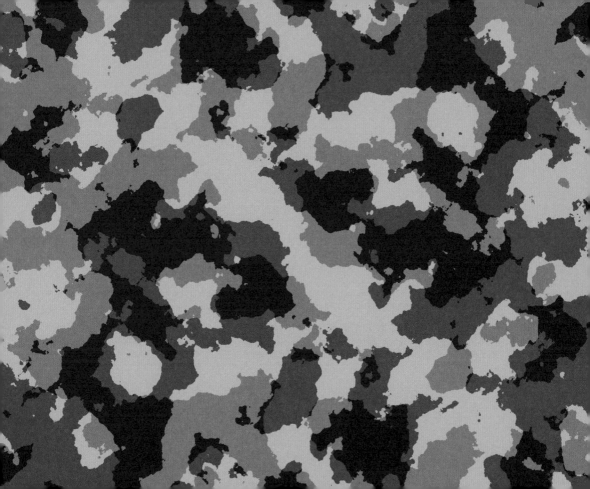

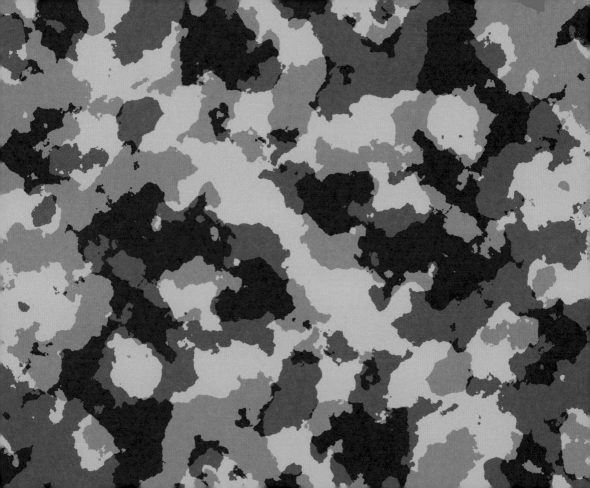

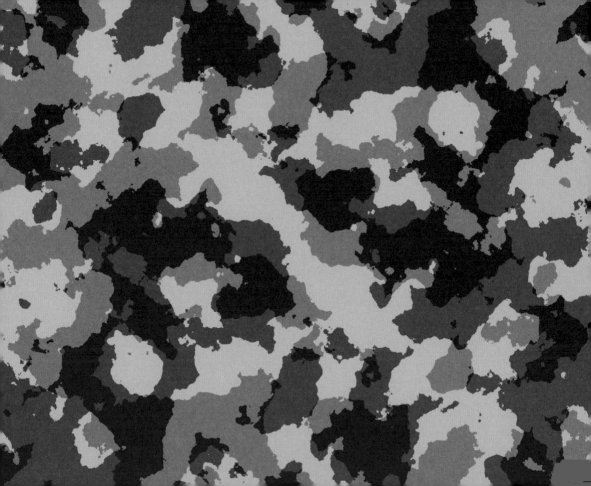

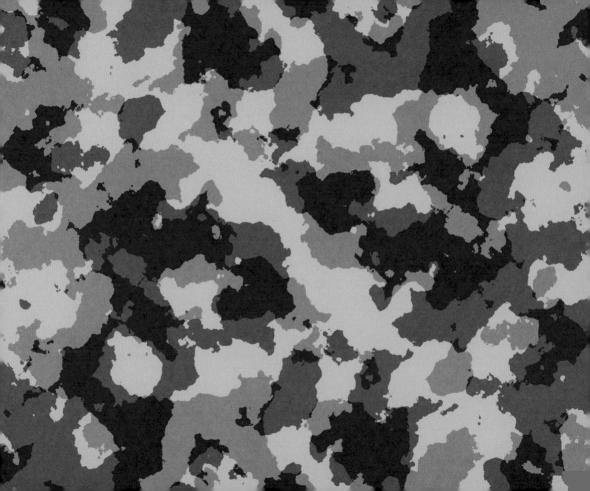

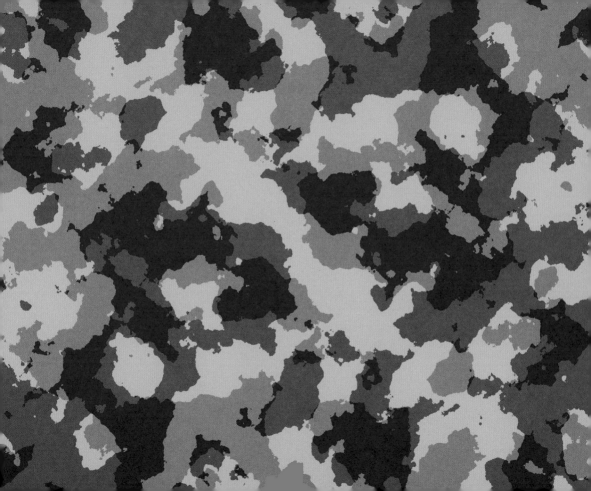

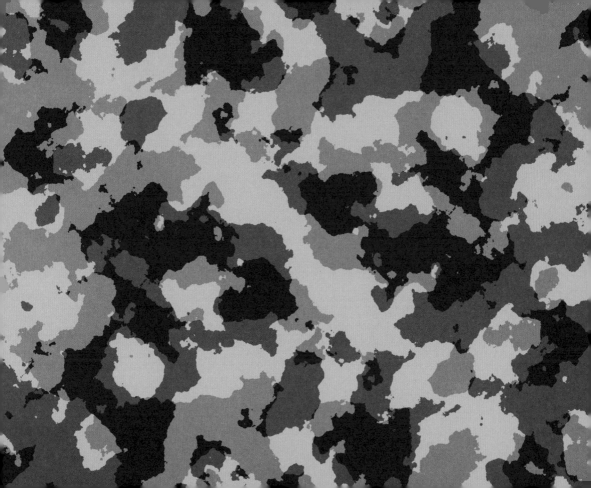

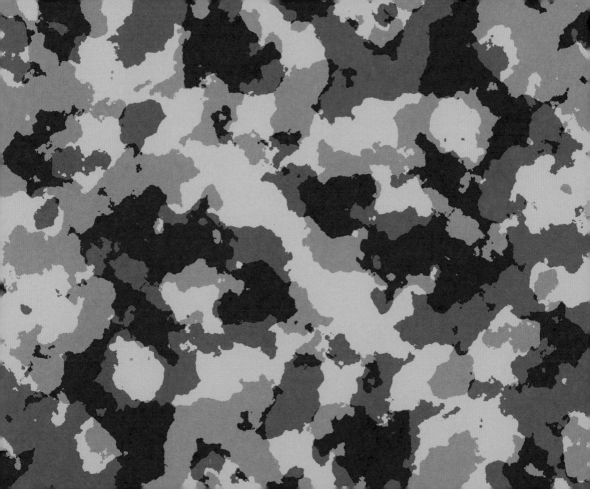

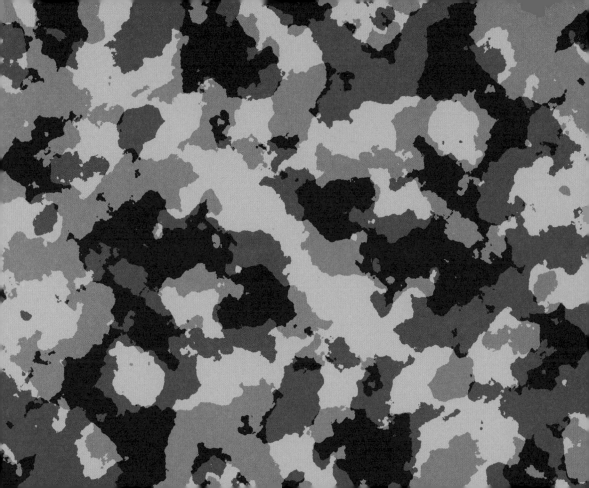

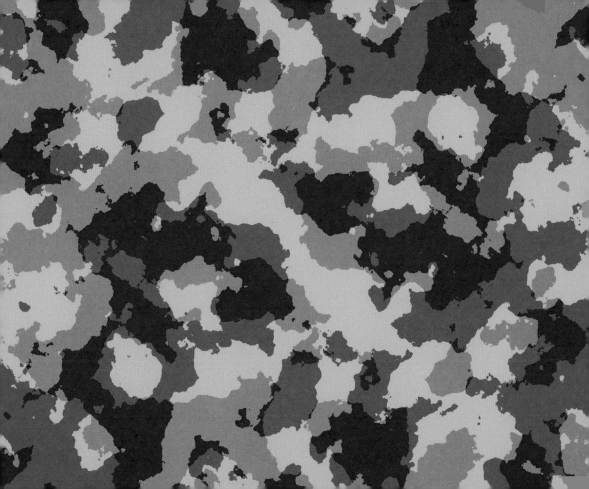

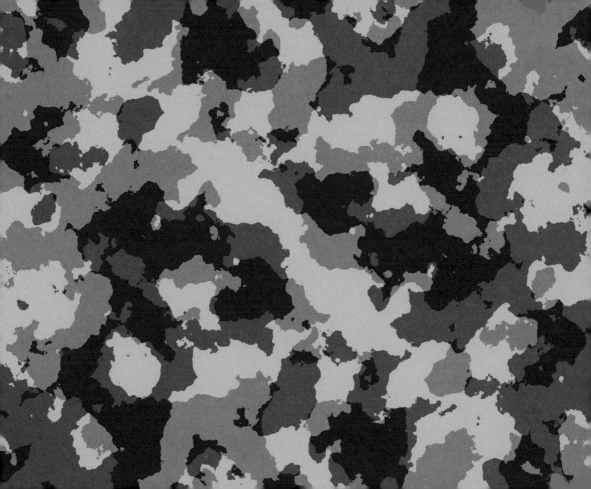

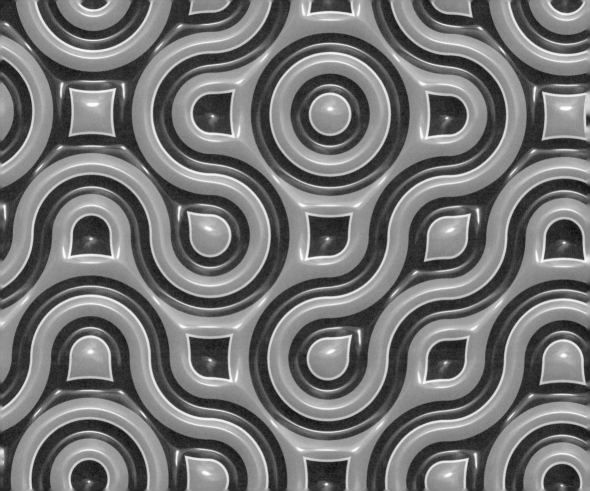

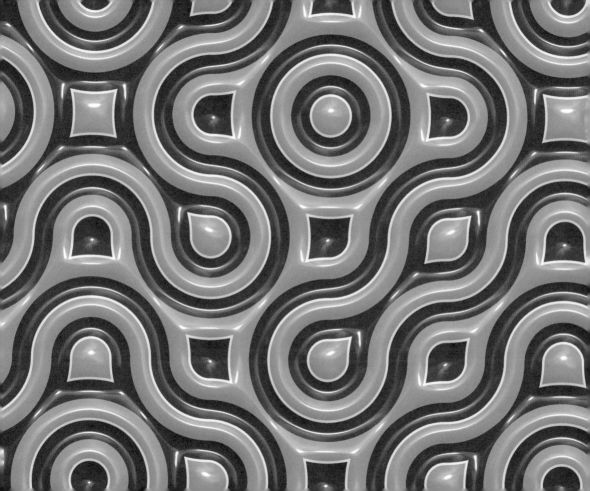

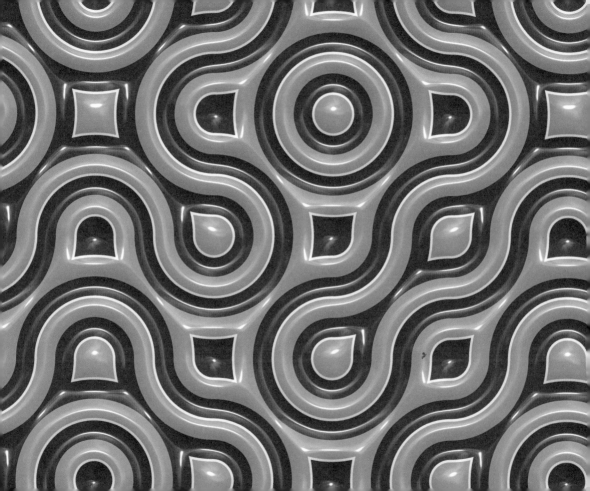

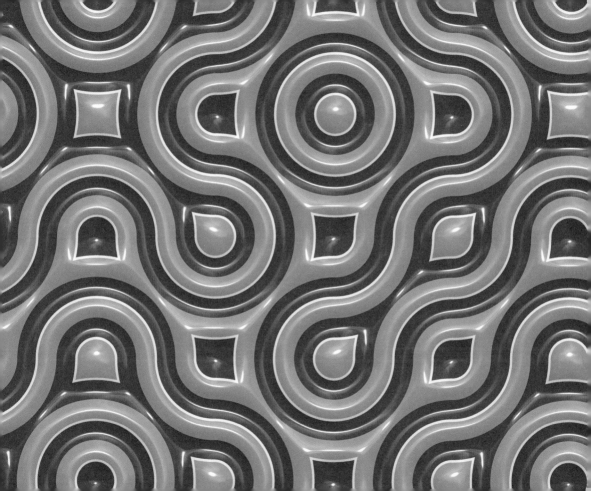

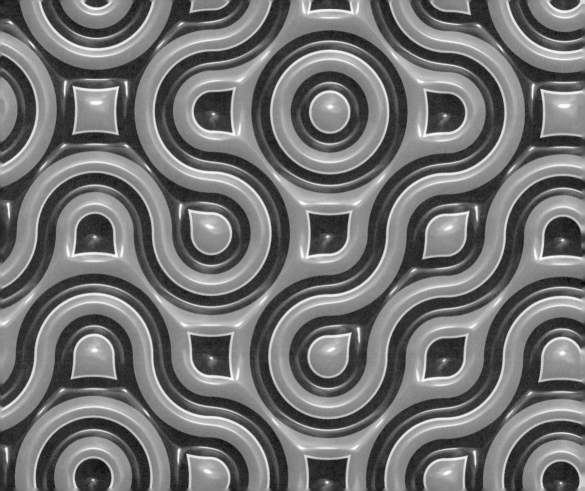

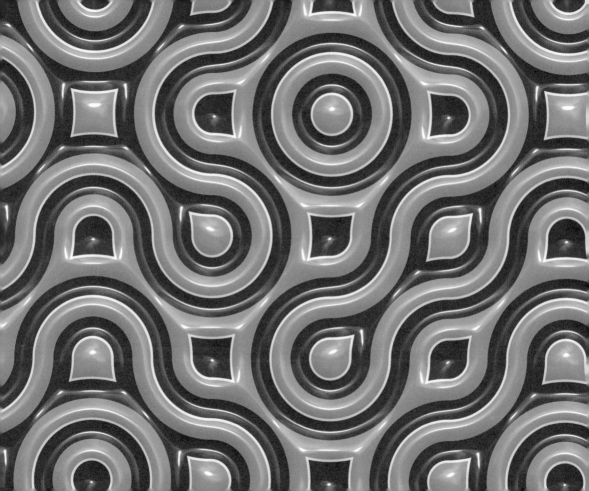

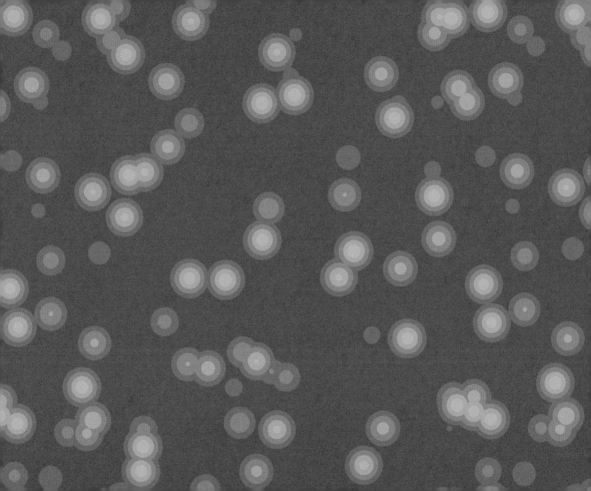

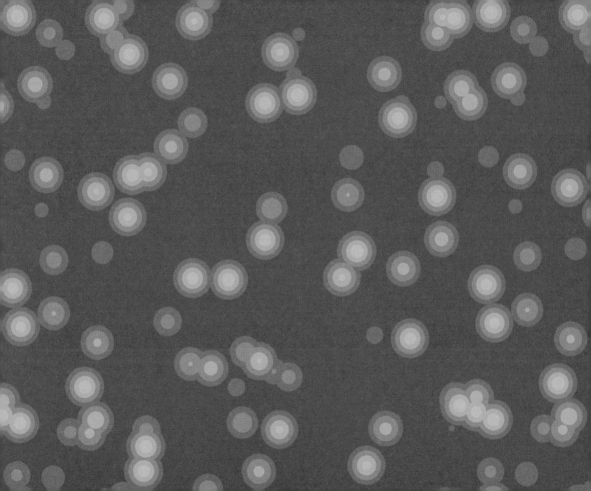

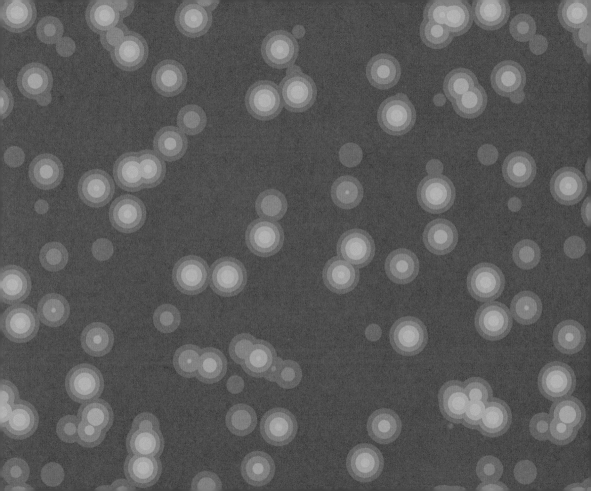

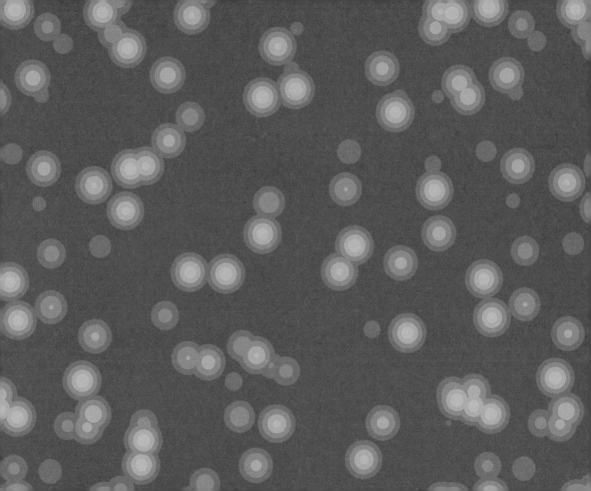

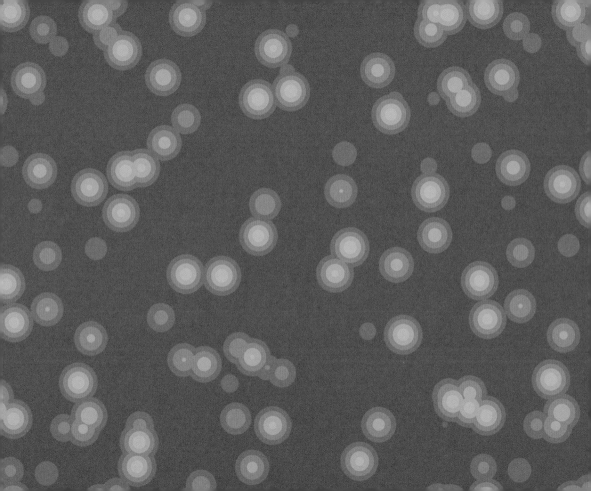

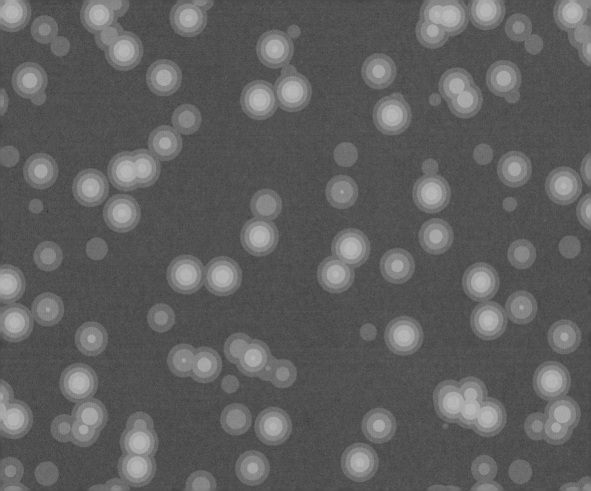

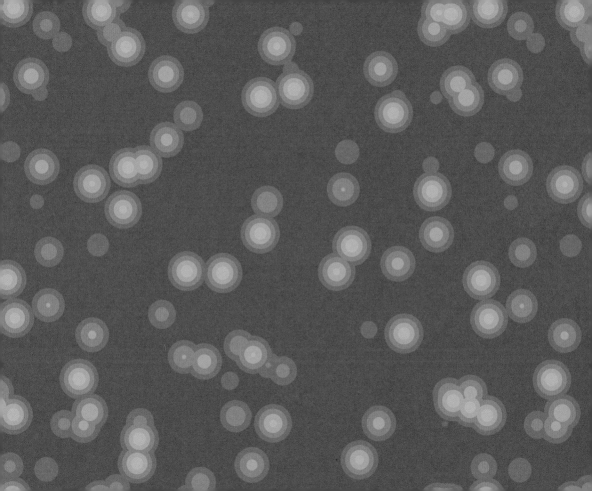

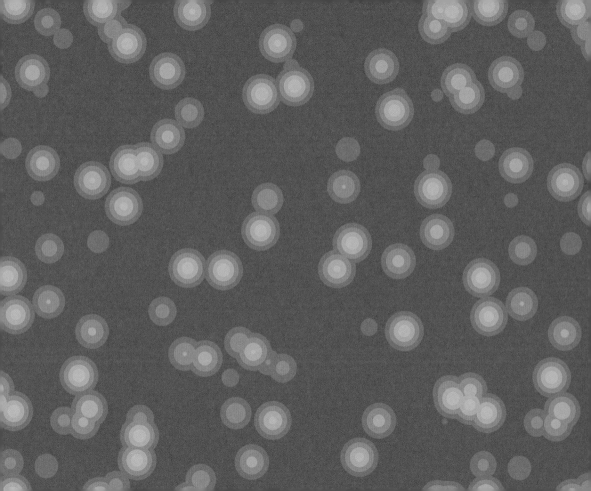

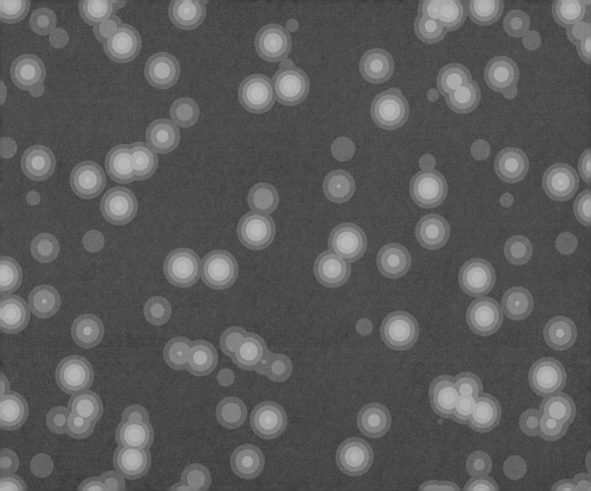

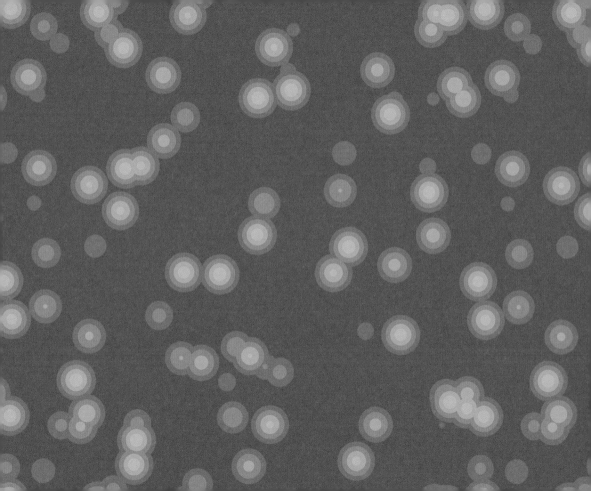

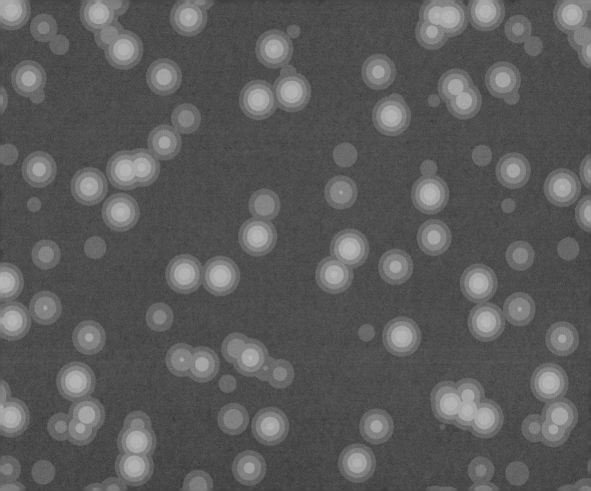

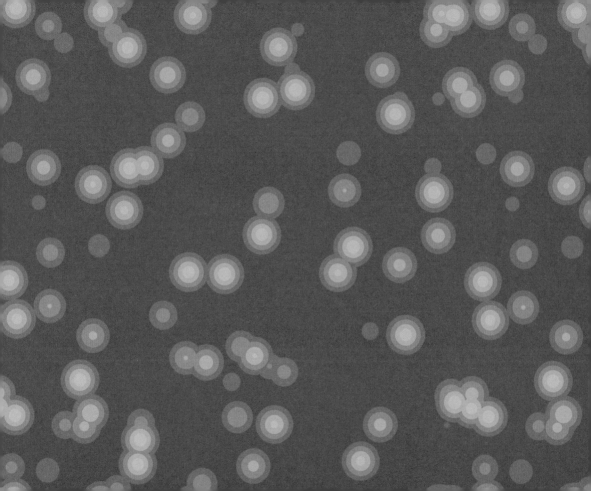

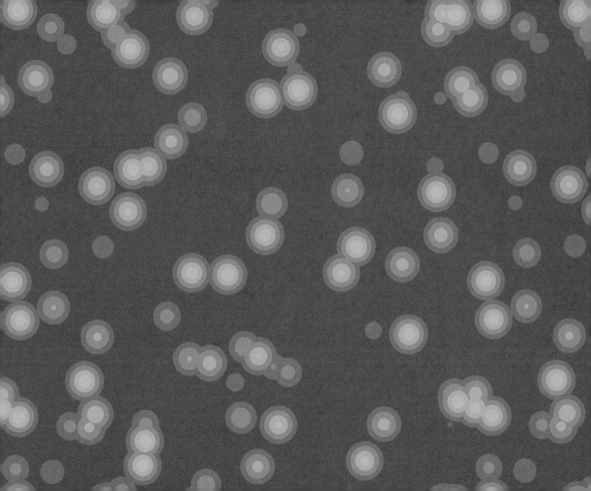

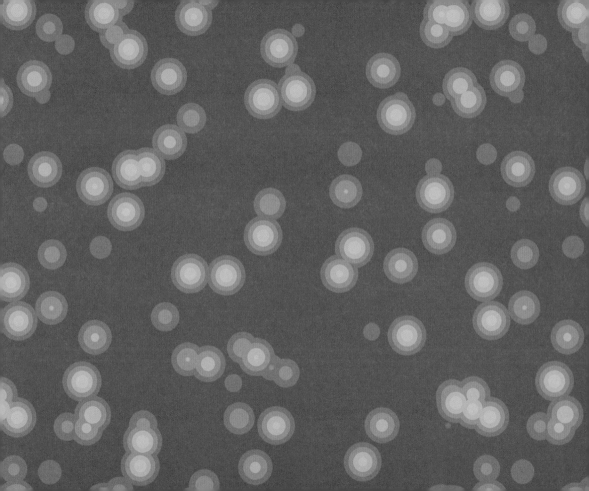

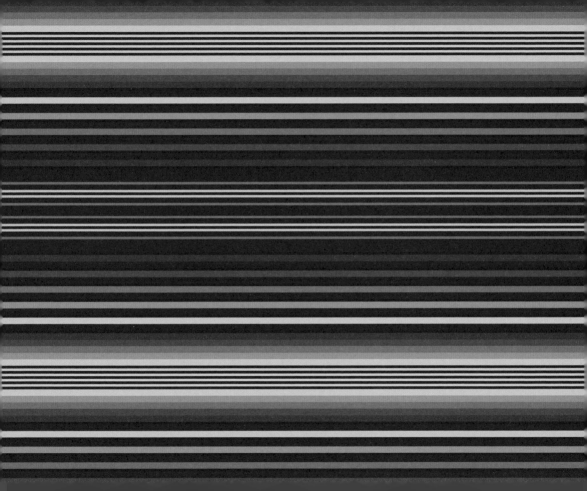

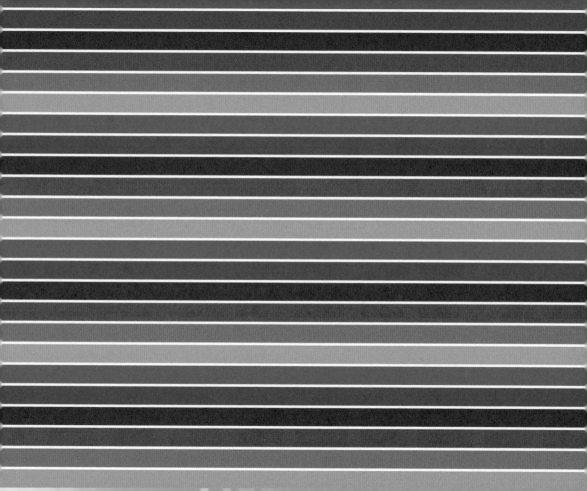

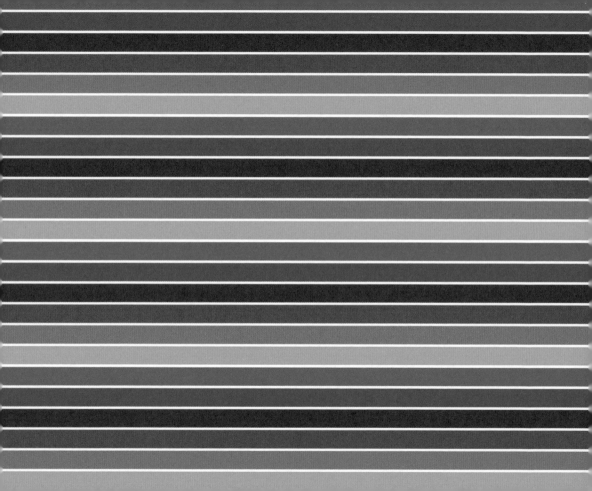

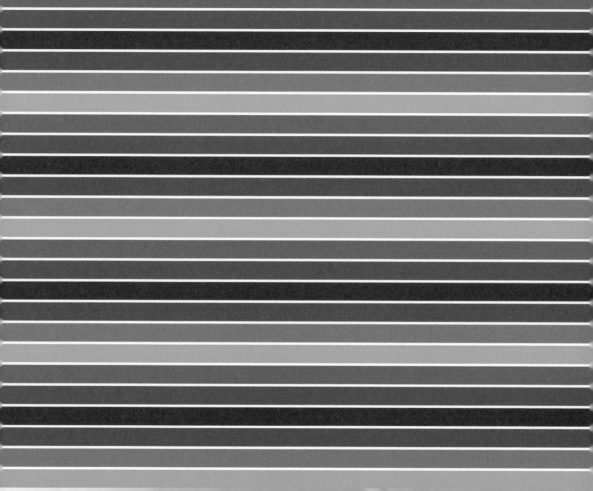

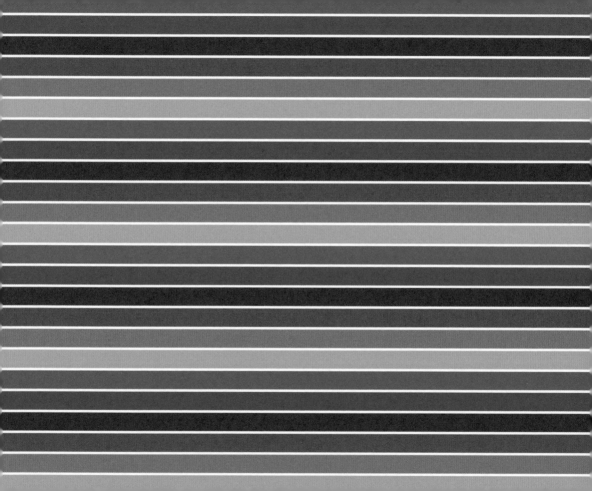

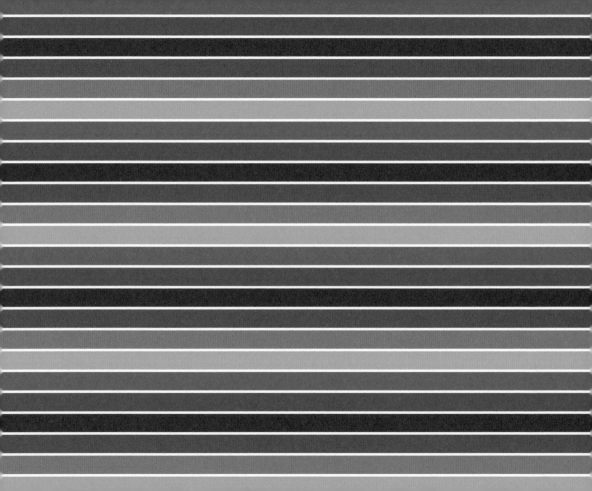

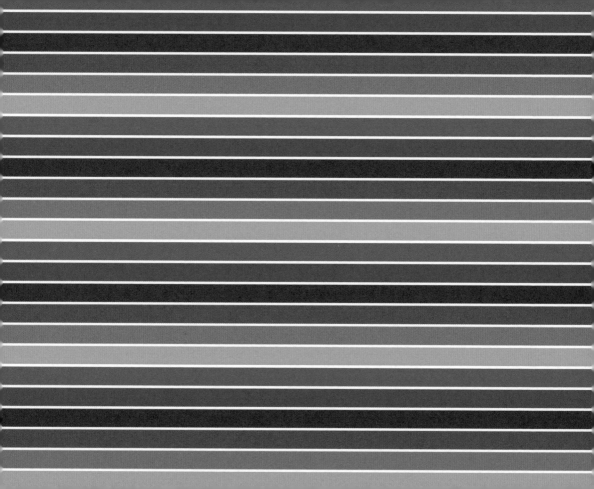

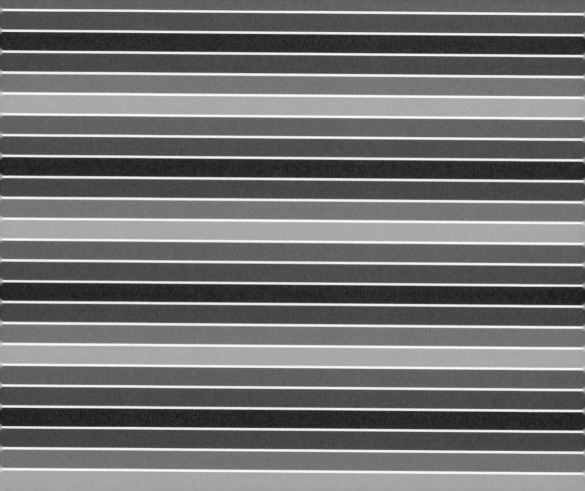

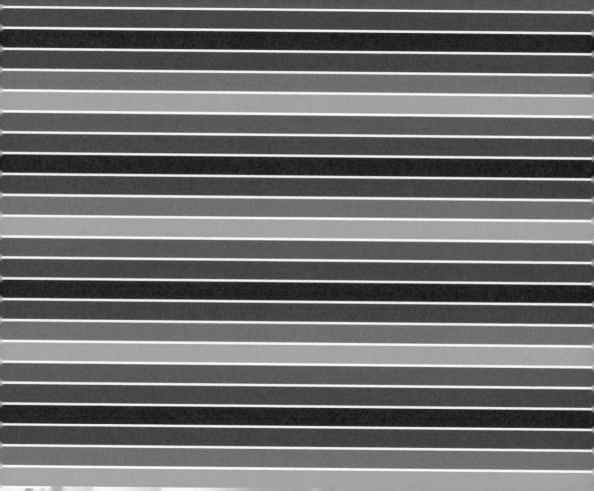

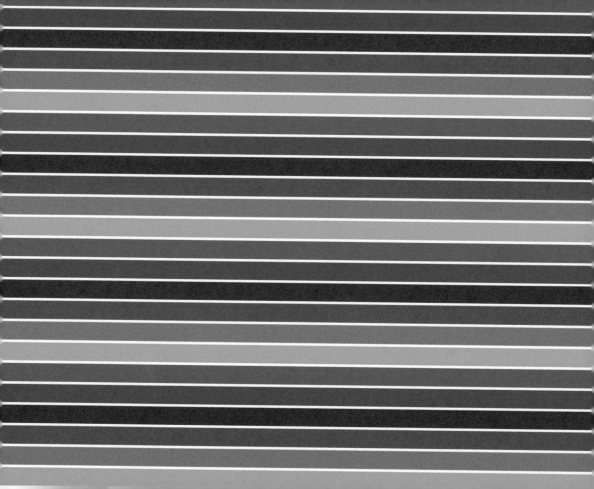

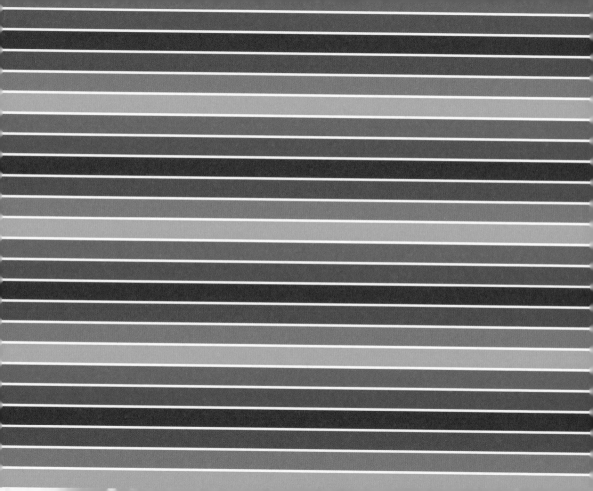

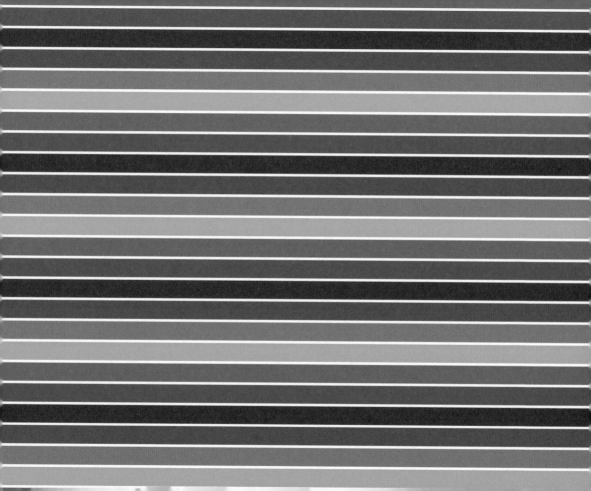

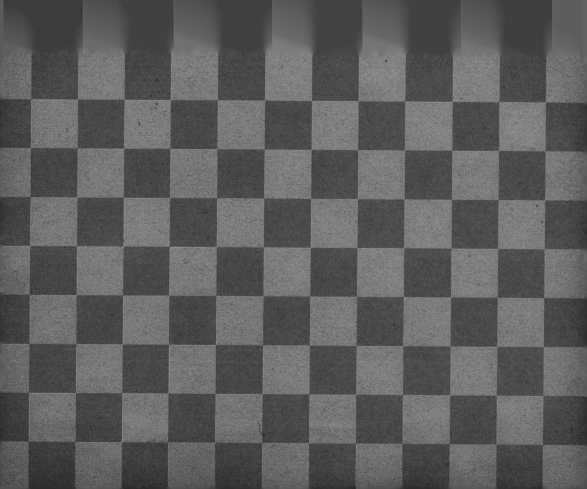

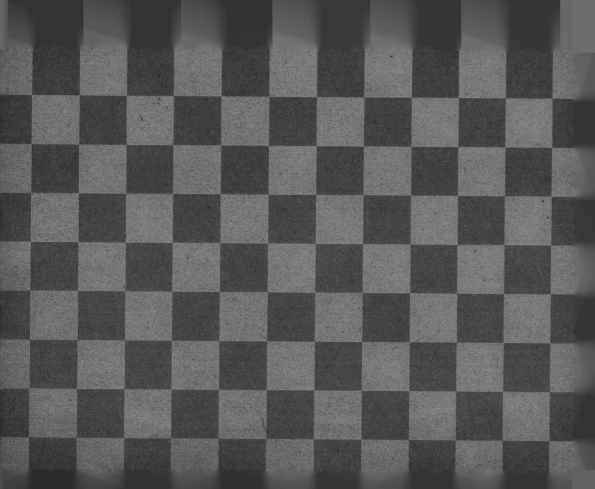

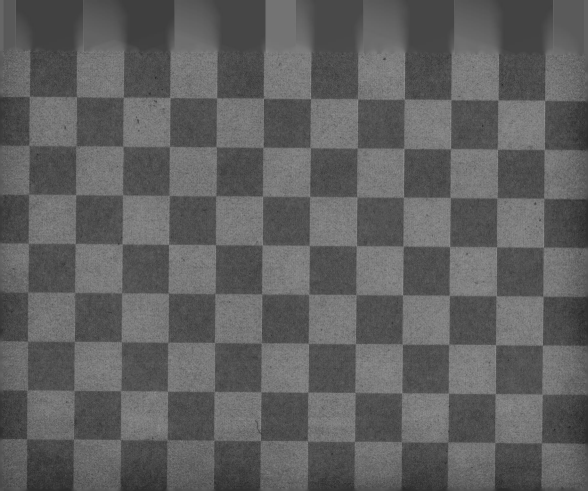

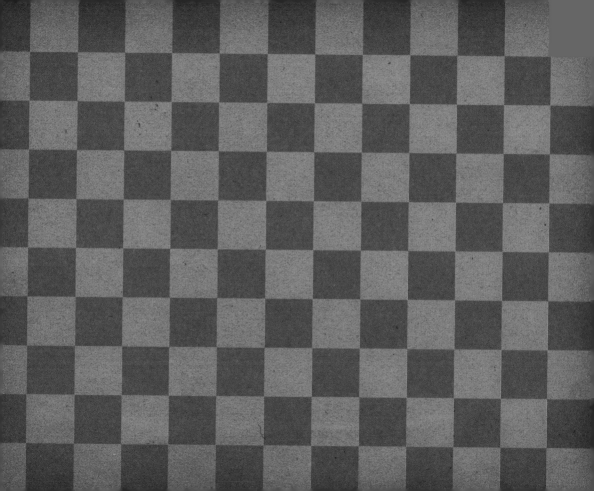

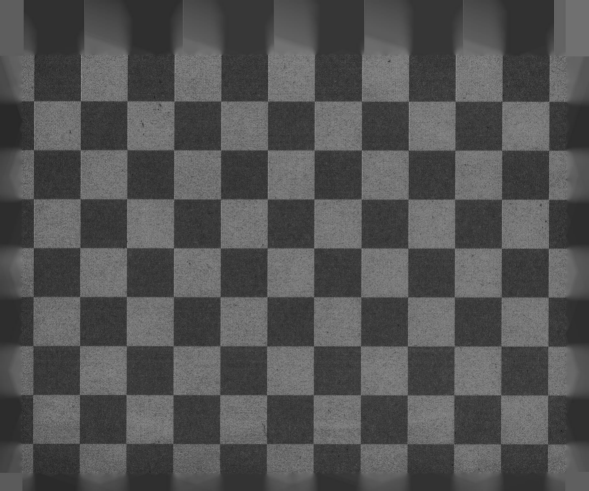

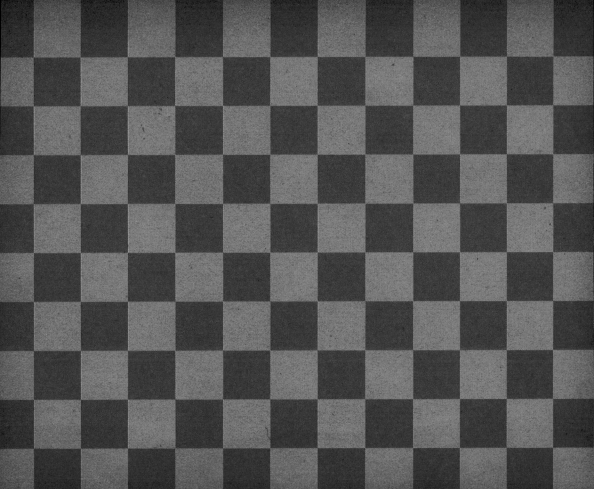

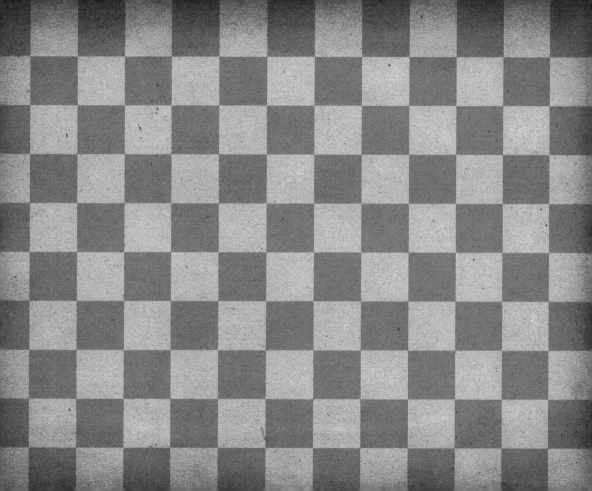

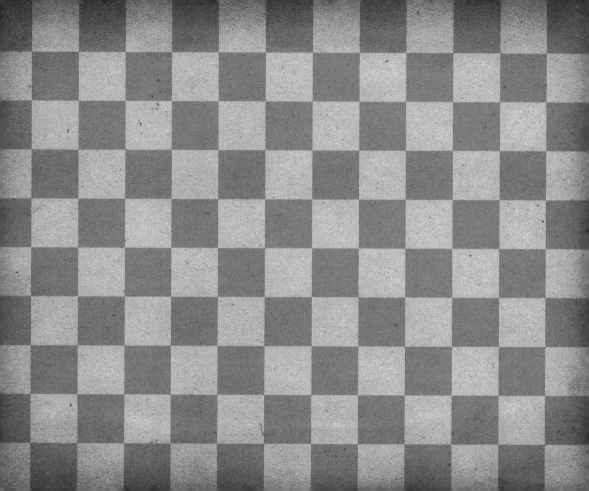

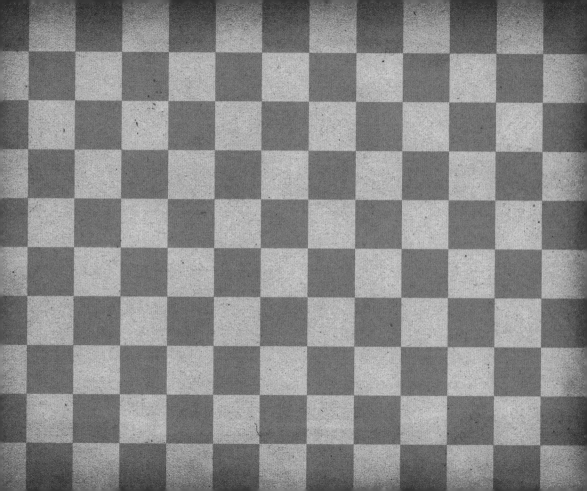

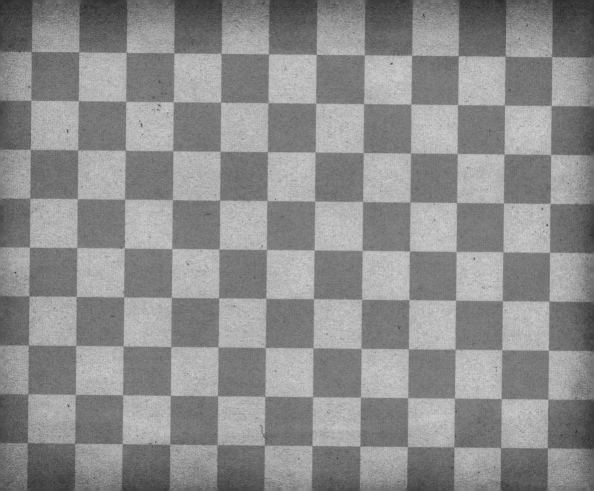

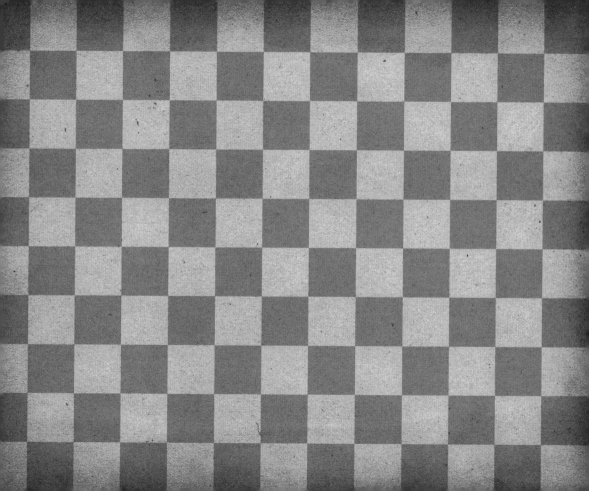

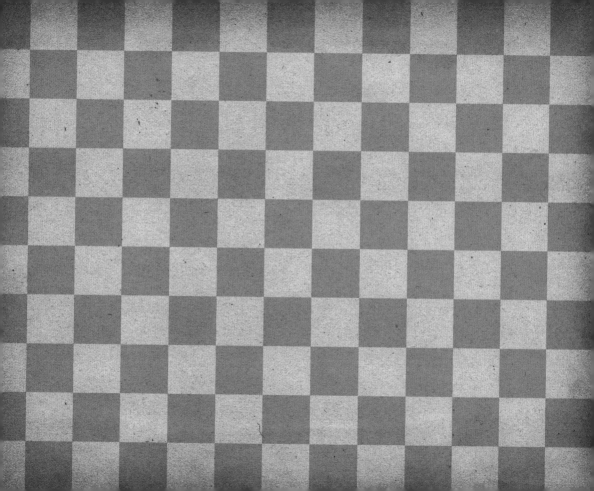

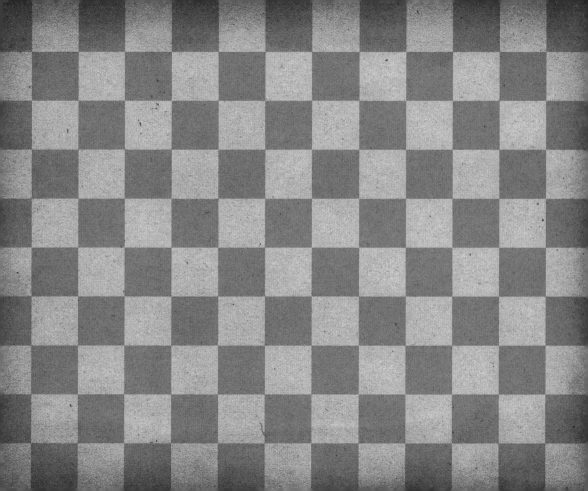

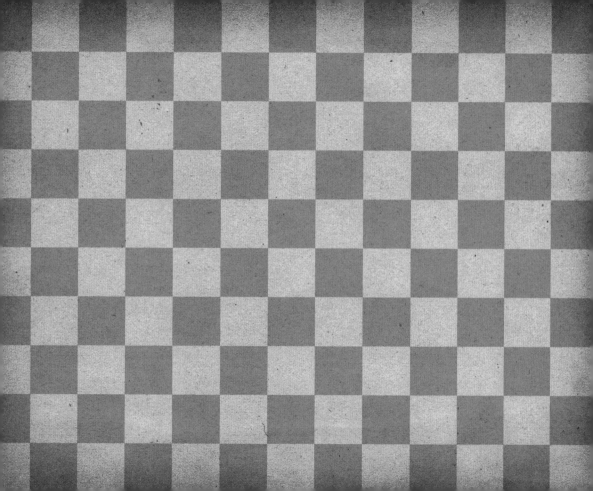

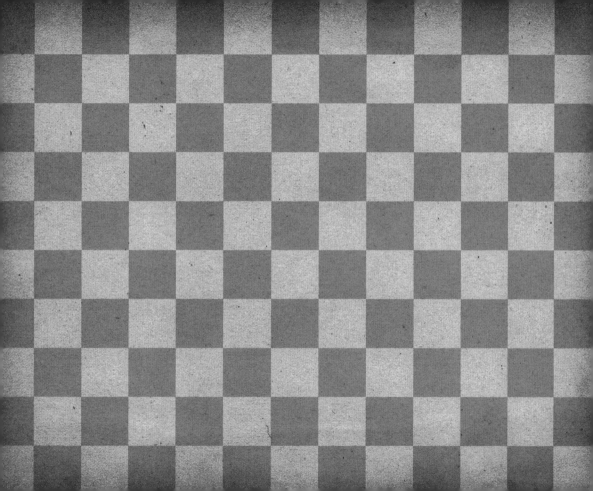

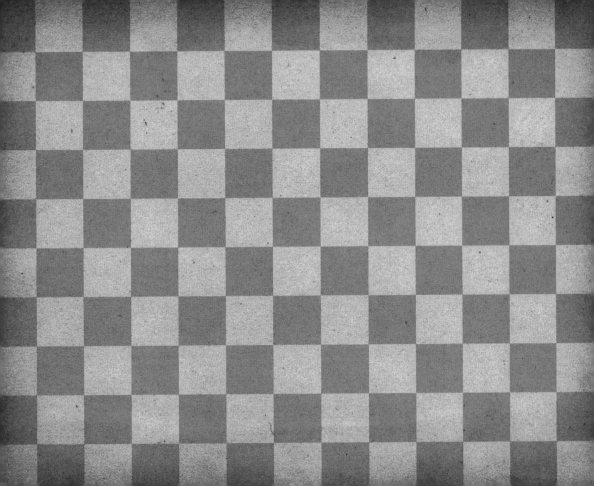

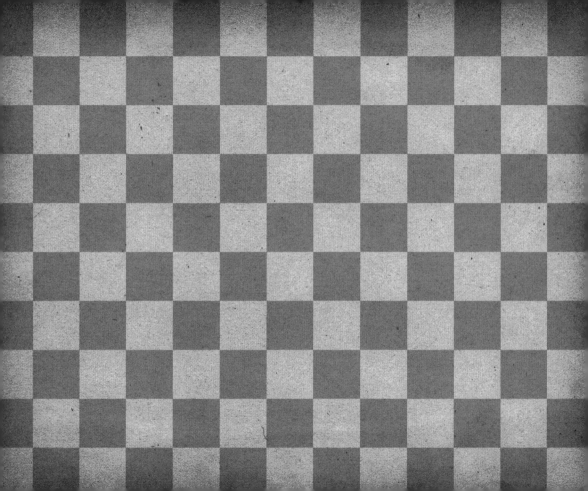

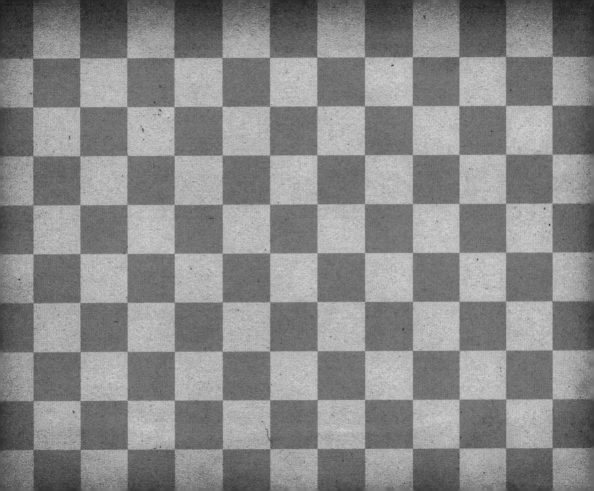

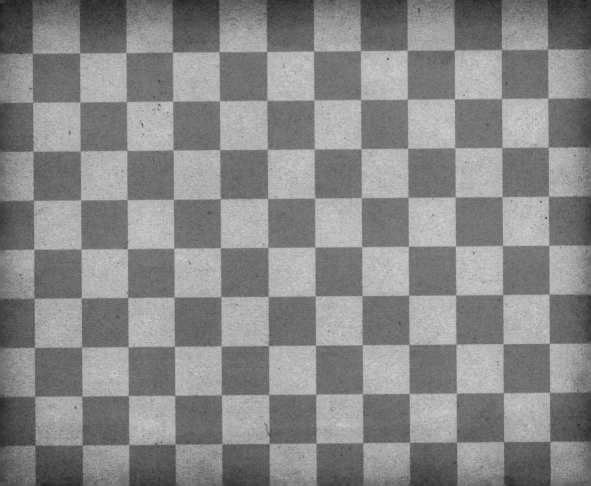

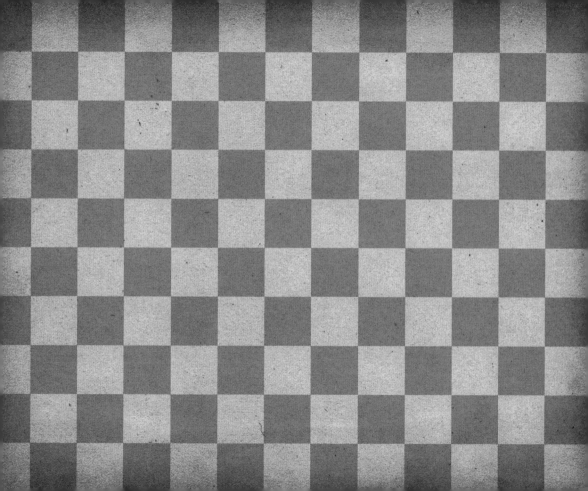

INDIAE ORIENTALIS, INSVLARVMQVE ADIACENTIVM TYPVS.

INDIAE
RIENTALIS,
VLARVMQVE
ACIENTI:
VM TY:
PVS.
SIAE
phorum Im
mites ad In
uium vsque
gunt
CARDANDAN
Dalanguer mons
Naugracot mons
Vsontz mons
AMERICAE, Siue Indię
Mare Cin
IAPAN.
Hanc insulam M. Paul. Venet Zipangri vocat.
OCEANVS
MANGI quę et CIN et CHINA.
MIEN.
TIPVRA
ARACAM.
INDOSTAN.
BENGALA
CAMBAIA
MANDAO
ORIXA
DELLI
DECAN
NARZINGA
BISINAGAR
Golfo di Bengala
Zeilan insula Tenarisim incolis dicta
Andramania id est aurea insula
VERMA
BREMA
PEGV
SIAN.
CAMBOIA
ÇAM
CACHV CHINA
Lequio maior
Lequio minor
Tropicus Cancri
ORIENTALIS
Los dos hermanos
Mindanao
Borneo ins.
Celebes
Circulus æquinoctialis.
Sumatra olim Taprobana
Malaca
IAVA MAIOR
Insulę Moluccę celebres ob maximam aromatum copiam, quam per totum terrarũ orbem transferunt, 5. sunt, iuxta Gilolo nempe Taranate, Tidore, Motir, Machiã et Bachiã.
NOVA GV
quam Andreas
ram Piccinaculi
detur. An insula
continentis Austr
tum est.

AMERICÆ, siue India
Delanguer mons
CARDANDAN.
Naugracot mons. Vssontic
mons
Mare Cin
Quisara
Sanderber

SIAE
phorum Im:
mites ad In:
uium usque
gunt

MANGI quæ et CIN
et CHINA
IAPAN.
OCEANVS

MIEN.
TIPVRA

ARACAM.
INDOS
TAN.

CAMBALA
MANDAO
ORIZA
BENGALA
DELLI
DE CAN.
MARZINGAR
DISINA
GAR

VERMA

BREMA
IAVA
PEGV
CAM

STAN.
CAMBOIA.

CACHV CHINA

ORIENTALIS

Tropicus Cancri

Les dos hermanos

Insulæ Moluccæ, celebres ob maxi
mã aromatum copiam, quam per
totum terrarum orbem trans
ferunt, sunt, quorum Globo
insertæ, nempe Tarenate, Tidore,
Motir, Machiā et Bachiā

Golfo di Bengala.

Borneo ins.

Circulus æquinoctialis.

INDIAE
RIENTALIS,
VLARVMQVE
IACIENTI:
VM TY:
PVS.

SVMA
TRA

IAVA MAIOR

CELEBES

NOVA G
quam Andreas
ram Piccinaculo
detur. An ĩ
continentis Au
tum est

INDIAE ORIENTALIS, INSVLARVMQVE ADIACIENTIVM TYPVS.

INDIAE ORIENTALIS, INSVLARVMQVE ADIACIENTIVM TYPVS

INDIAE ORIENTALIS, INSVLARVMQVE ADIACENTIVM TYPVS.

INDIAE ORIENTALIS, INSVLARVMQVE ADIACENTIVM TYPVS.

Dalanguer mons · CARDANDAN · *Naugracot mons* · *Vssonte mons* · *Mare Cin*

AMERICAE, Siue Indiæ

SIAE phorum Inſmites ad Inuium vſque gunt

MIEN.

MANGI quæ et CIN. et CHINA.

IAPAN.

OCEANVS

Hanc inſulam M. Paul. Venet Zipangri vocat.

Las dos hermanas

STIFVRA

ARA CAM.

INDOSTAN.

BENGALA.

CAMBAL

ORIXA

CANDAO

DELLI

DE CIN.

Tropicus Cancri

CACHV CHINA.

ORIENTALIS

NARZINGA

BISNA GAR.

VERMA

BREMA.

PEGV

SIAN

CAMBOIA.

Golfo di Bengala

Humanu vel yⁿ di buoni ſegni

Zamij

Cenalo

Abarim Humanan

yᵉ de ſaos loles

yᵉ de arreciſes

yᵉ de cocos

Mindanao

Iſulæ Moluccæ celebres ob maxiⁿ aromatum copiam, quam per totum terrarū orbem tranſferunt, ſ. ſunt, ſcilicet Gilolo, nempe Tarenate, Tidore, Motir, Machali et Bachili.

Circulus æquinoctialis.

Borneo inſ.

Celebes

IAVA MAIOR

NOVA GV quam Andreas C ram Piccinacli ap detur. An inſula continentis Auſtrtum eſt.

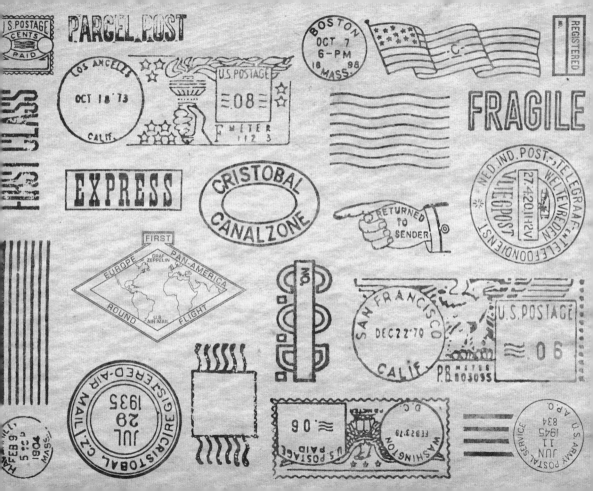

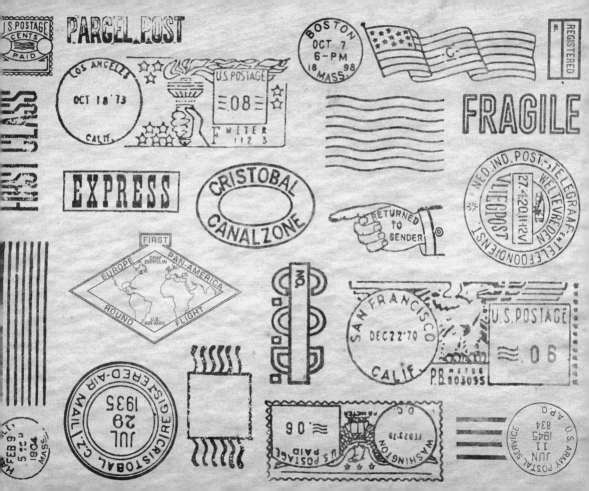

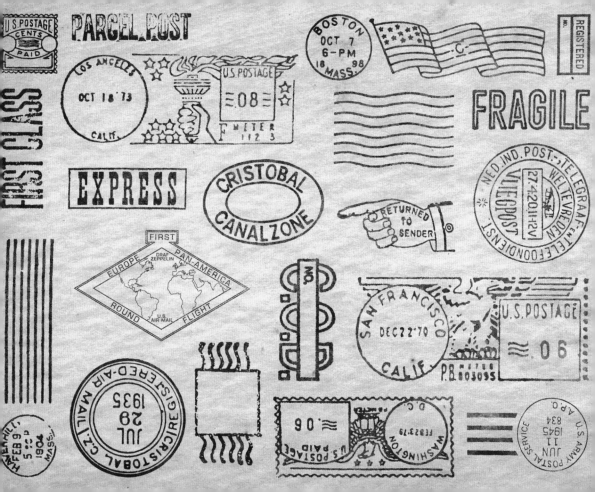

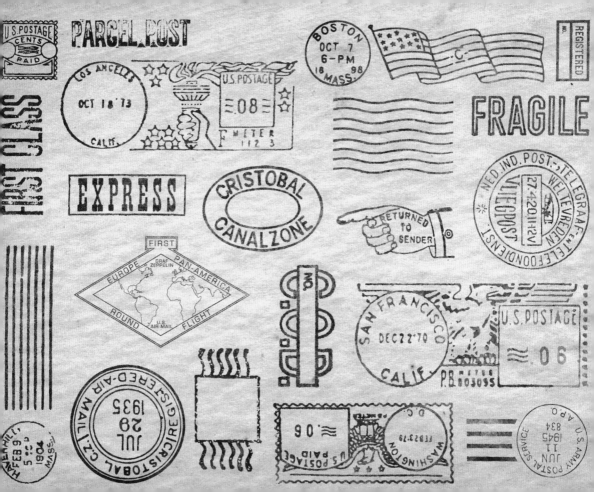

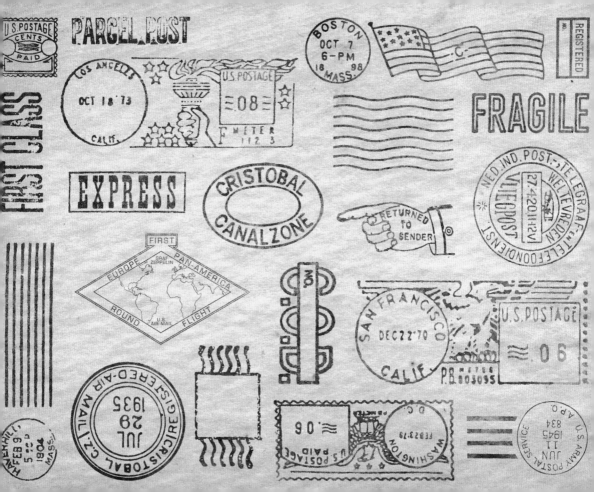

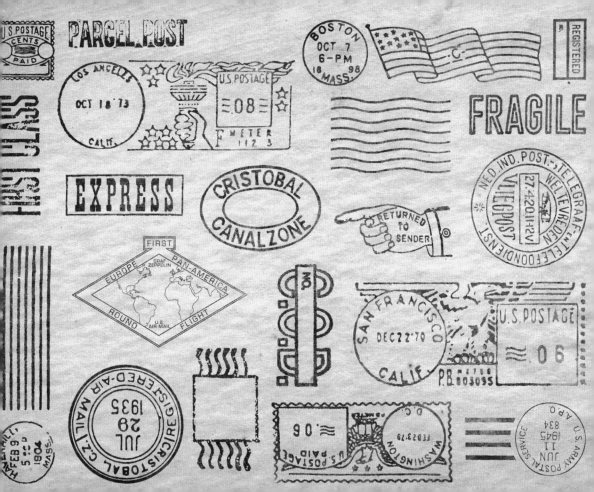

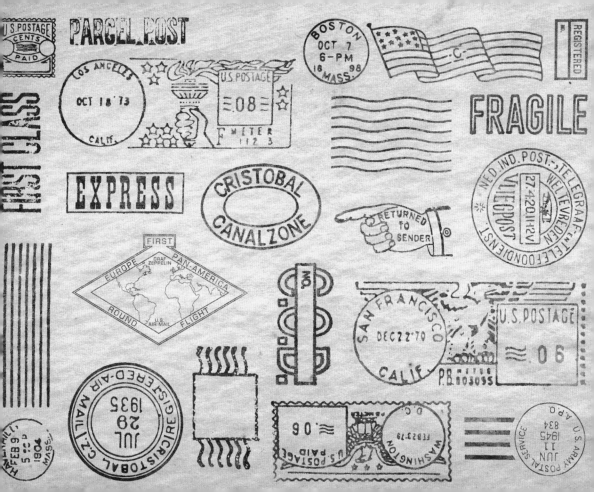

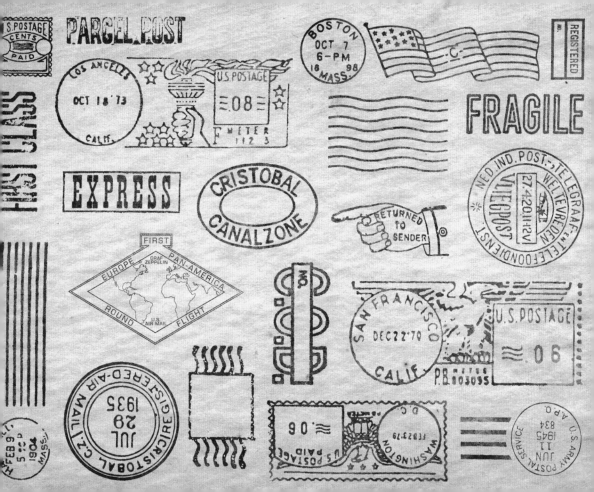

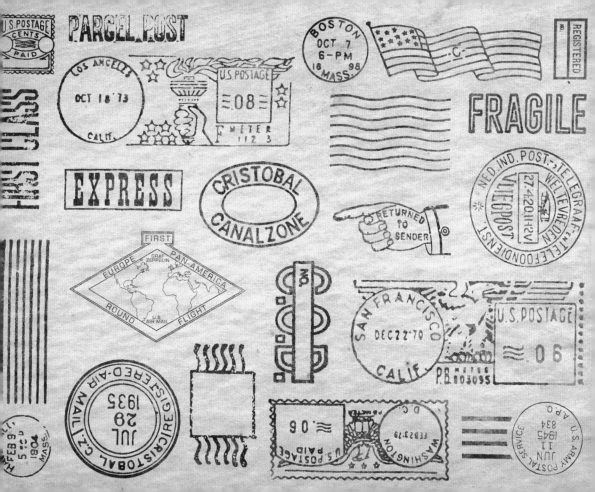

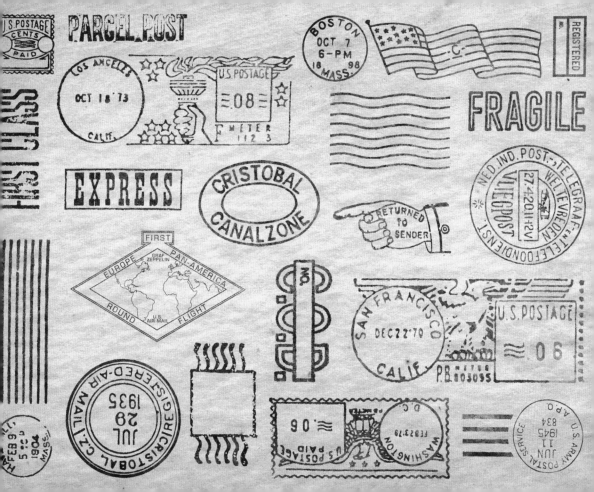

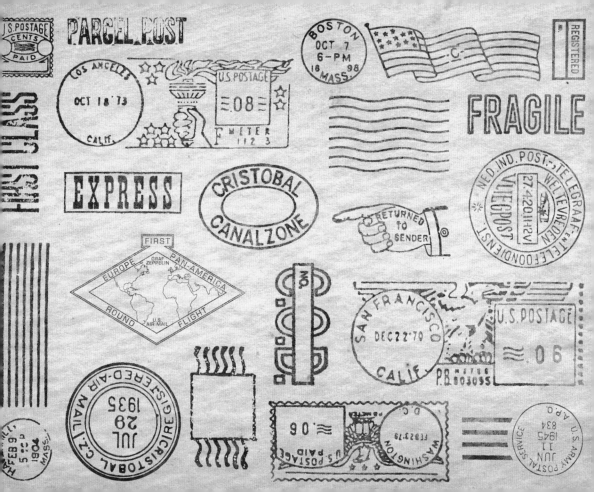

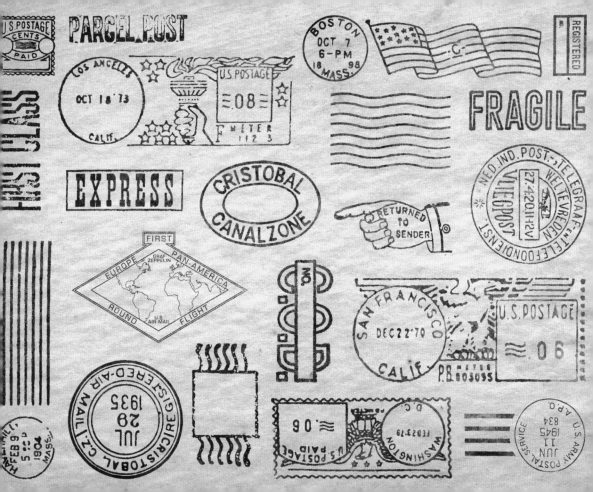

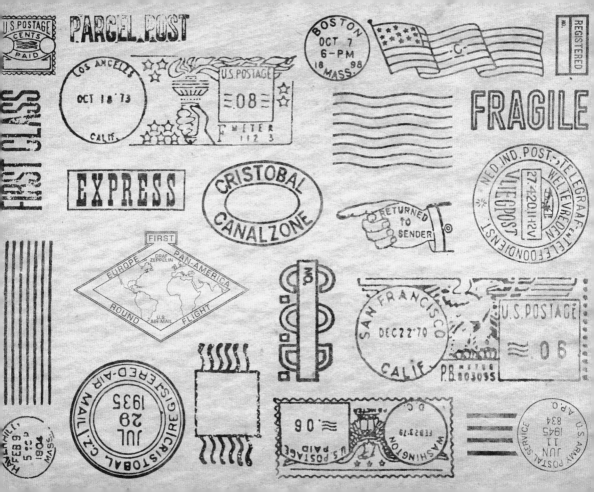